371.2

Every Child Matters
A Practical Guide for Teachers

Loughborough College

LC052399

Also available:

Every Child Matters
A New Role for SENCOs
Rita Cheminais
1-84312-406-8

Every Child Matters
A Practical Guide for Teachers

RITA CHEMINAIS

 David Fulton Publishers

This edition reprinted 2010 by Routledge
2 Park Square, Milton Park, Abingdon, Oxon, OX14 4RN
Simultaneously published in the USA and Canada by Routledge
270 Madison Avenue, New York, NY 10016

First published in Great Britain in 2006 by David Fulton Publishers

Reprinted 2006, 2008

10 9

Copyright © Rita Cheminais 2006

Note: The right of Rita Cheminais to be identified as the authors of this work has been asserted by her in accordance with the Copyright, Designs and Patents Act 1988

British Library Cataloguing in Publication Data
A catalogue record for this book is available from the British Library.

ISBN: 1 84312 463 7
EAN: 978 1 84312 463 4

All rights reserved. No part of this may be reproduced, stored in a retrieval system or transmitted, in any form or by any means, electronic, mechanical, photocopying, or otherwise, without the prior permission of the publishers.

Typeset by FiSH Books, Enfield, Middx.
Printed and bound in Great Britain

Contents

List of Figures and Tables

Figures

Tables

Acknowledgements

Thanks are due to colleagues around the country whom I have had the pleasure to meet while on my travels to a number of local authorities, who have highlighted the urgent need for awareness raising, and for a practical resource for qualified and trainee teachers in schools on the *Every Child Matters* Change for Children programme, in order to prepare them for their new and changing role.

Special thanks go to:

all the senior managers and teachers I have worked with in schools, who have helped me to identify what the key issues and complexities are in managing rapid change on a personal and whole-school level;

Philip Eastwood, who for many years has given me the encouragement, inspiration and ideas to write practical resources for teachers;

Linda Evans, my previous commissioning editor with David Fulton Publishers, for her continual belief in my work; and

last, but not least, Tracey Alcock, my current commissioning editor with David Fulton Publishers, for her enthusiasm, invaluable guidance and advice in putting this book together.

While every effort has been made to acknowledge sources throughout the book, such is the range of aspects covered that I may have unintentionally omitted to mention their origin. If so, I offer my apologies to all concerned.

Abbreviations

AEN	additional educational needs
ASD	autistic spectrum disorder
AST	Advanced Skills Teacher
BESD	behavioural, emotional and social difficulties
BEST	Behaviour and Education Support Team
BIP	Behaviour Improvement Programme
CAF	Common Assessment Framework
CAMHS	Child and Adolescent Mental Health Service
CLC	City Learning Centre
CP	Child Protection
CPD	continuing professional development
CRB	Criminal Records Bureau
CSIE	Centre for Studies in Inclusive Education
DfES	Department for Education and Skills
DH	Department of Health
EAL	English as an additional language
EBD	emotional and behavioural difficulties
ECM	*Every Child Matters*
EiC	Excellence in Cities
EIP	Education Improvement Partnership
EMA	ethnic minority achievement
FFT	Fischer Family Trust
FSM	free school meals
GCSE	General Certificate of Secondary Education
GNVQ	General National Vocational Qualification
GP	General Practitioner
G&T	gifted and talented
GTC	General Teaching Council
HE	Higher Education
HLTA	higher level teaching assistant
HMI	Her Majesty's Inspector
ICT	information and communication technology
IEP	Individual Education Plan
INCO	inclusion co-ordinator
INSET	in-service education and training
IRSC	Investigation and Referral Support Co-ordinators
IS	information sharing
ITT	Initial Teacher Training
KS	key stage
LA	local authority

LAC	looked after children
LDD	learning difficulties and/or disabilities
LSA	learning support assistant
MLD	moderate learning difficulties
NCSL	National College for School Leadership
NHS	National Health Service
NQT	newly qualified teacher
NRwS	New Relationship with Schools
NSF	National Service Framework
OFSTED	Office for Standards in Education
PANDA	Performance and Assessment Report
PAT	Pupil Achievement Tracker
PD	physical disabilities
PE	physical education
PIVATS	Performance Indicators for Value Added Target Setting
PMLD	profound, multiple learning difficulties
PPA	planning, preparation and assessment
PRU	Pupil Referral Unit
PSHE	Personal, Social and Health Education
PTA	Parent Teacher Association
QCA	Qualifications and Curriculum Authority
QTS	Qualified Teacher Status
RBA	*Removing Barriers to Achievement*
SCT	School Change Team
SEF	self-evaluation form
SEN	special educational needs
SENCO	special educational needs co-ordinator
SHA	Secondary Headteachers Association
SIP	School Improvement Partner
SLCN	speech, language and communication needs
SLD	severe learning difficulties
SMART	specific, measurable, achievable, relevant, time-related
SPLD	specific learning difficulties
SWOT	strengths, weaknesses, opportunities and threats
TA	teaching assistant
TDA	Training and Development Agency
TPLF	*Teachers' Professional Learning Framework*
TTA	Teacher Training Agency
VAK	visual, auditory, kinaesthetic

The Aim of this Book

The aim of this book is to enable teachers working in a range of educational settings from Foundation Stage through to Key Stage 4 to know:

- what their role and expectations are in the light of the government's programme for change;
- how to meet the *Every Child Matters* five well-being outcomes for children and young people;
- how to remove barriers to achievement in personalising learning approaches;
- how to self-review, monitor and evaluate the *Every Child Matters* five outcomes for children, aligned to the OFSTED inspection framework;
- how to work in partnership with other paraprofessionals from within school, and from external services.

Who the book is for:

- all teachers;
- trainee and newly qualified teachers (NQTs);
- NQT Induction Tutors and Advanced Skills Teachers, Excellent Teachers;
- senior managers in schools;
- local authority advisers, inspectors or consultants responsible for supporting and training teachers, including NQTs;
- Senior Lecturers in Higher Education Institutions providing ongoing training for Initial Teacher Training, NQTs and experienced teachers;
- all other professionals from education, health and social care services planning courses and delivering training programmes to trainee and qualified teachers.

How the format is designed to be used

The book provides a resource that can be used:

- to act as a point of quick reference for trainee and qualified teachers, and senior managers, including NQT induction tutors in schools;
- to inform more responsive inclusive classroom practice;
- to enable pages to be photocopied for developmental purposes, within the purchasing institution or service.

Introduction

Schools are changing rapidly. The pace of change is fast and schools in the twenty-first century are adopting new ways of working to raise children's achievement and improve their well-being and life chances. All teachers now, and in the future, need to be well equipped to meet the demands of inclusive education.

Teachers make a significant contribution and difference to every child's life. By 2006, there will be a 'full-service' extended school in every local authority (LA) in England. The government is helping schools to deliver services such as health care, family learning and after-school activities, as well as building closer partnership links with a range of children's services in the local community.

In *Removing Barriers to Achievement* the government acknowledged that trainee and newly qualified teachers would benefit from increased input during Initial Teacher Training and induction in relation to inclusion, curriculum access, behaviour management, emotional well-being and assessment for learning. This would prepare and equip them, like all teachers, to:

> have the skills and confidence – and access to specialist advice where necessary – to help children to reach their potential.
>
> (DfES 2004m: 3.10)

Every Child Matters: Change for Children in Schools (DfES 2004e) identifies that pupil performance and well-being go hand in hand. Children and young people cannot learn if they do not feel safe or if health problems create barriers. The five outcomes for children and young people are central to ensuring that effective joined-up children's services from education, health and social care, provide 'wraparound' care in and on the site of schools, ensuring that children:

- are healthy;
- stay safe;
- enjoy and achieve;
- make a positive contribution;
- achieve economic and social well-being.

Every Child Matters (ECM) makes a significant commitment to the nurturing and education of the whole child. As schools adopt more of a multi-agency focus they will no longer be the sole site for, and provider of, learning, but instead, become gateways to a network of learning opportunities and activities provided by other local schools, colleges, distance learning programmes, e-learning and private companies, working across networked fully inclusive lifelong learning communities. Teachers will become facilitators, supporters and promoters of children's personalised learning and well-being, whereby pupils will achieve the best they can through working in a way that suits them. Personalised schools offering personalised learning opportunities and personalised services to meet the needs of the local community will become the future reality. Teachers working in future educational settings will adopt a more holistic approach, focused on the whole child's well-being, and not solely on his/her learning.

New role for classroom teachers

Transforming learning communities through Children's Centres, Full-Service Extended Schools, specialist schools, Academies, city learning centres and foundation partnerships will require teachers to be a:

- facilitator of pupils' personalised learning to meet a diversity of additional educational needs;
- remover of barriers to achievement and participation to enhance curriculum access and out-of-hours learning opportunities;
- supporter of pupils' emotional and physical well-being, good behaviour and achievement;
- advocate for children, safeguarding and promoting their welfare;
- promoter of equal opportunities, inclusion and equal access to extended school opportunities;
- champion for children, empowering and enabling pupils' 'voice' and their self-review on the *Every Child Matters* five outcomes for children;
- implementer of appropriate assessment for learning and analysis of pupil level data;
- reflective practitioner, solution focused enquirer, solving problems and informing decision-making;
- quality assurer, monitoring and evaluating the impact of teaching and other additional interventions on pupils' outcomes;
- contributor to inter-professional collaborative working partnerships, deploying teaching assistants and other paraprofessionals effectively within the classroom;
- contributor to networked learning communities;
- supporter of lifelong learning, family learning and parent partnership.

Every Child Matters strongly supports the principle of personalisation and acknowledges the work being done by schools already in this area:

- schools offering a range of extended services that help pupils engage and achieve, and build stronger relationships with parents and the wider community;
- supporting closer working between schools and specialist services to promote children's welfare, to safeguard children from abuse and neglect, so that children with additional needs can be identified earlier and supported effectively.

Children, young people and their parents and carers will become more active participants in the shaping, development and delivery of education and related personalised services in schools and Children's Centres. In *Removing Barriers to Achievement* the government emphasises:

> All children have the right to a good education and the opportunity to fulfil their potential. All teachers should expect to teach children with special educational needs and all schools should play their part in educating children from the local community, whatever their background or ability.
>
> (DfES 2004m: Introduction)

As reflective practitioners working in the context of *Every Child Matters*, teachers need to answer the following key questions:

- Do I think this pupil is making sufficient progress towards meeting the five outcomes of *Every Child Matters* successfully?
- If not, then what can I do to improve the well-being and learning opportunities for that child or young person in my class?

1

Change for Children Programme: Opportunities and Challenges for Teachers

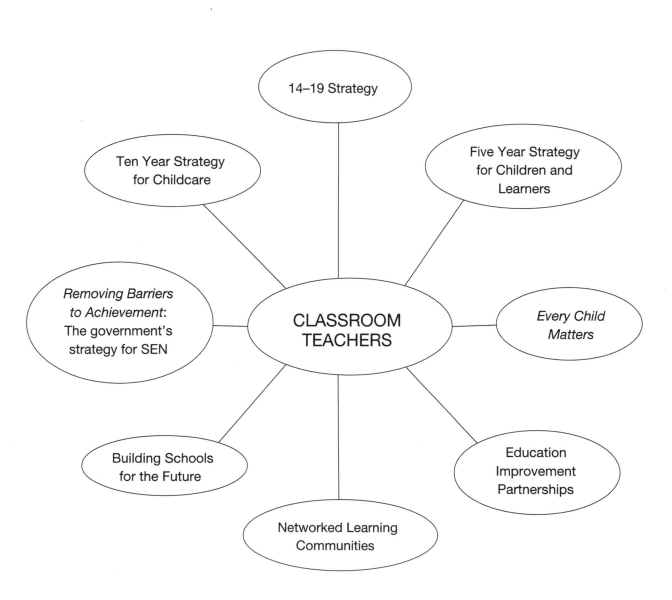

New opportunities for teachers

In the context of the current government's programme of change, the traditional role of the classroom teacher needs reconfiguring and re-conceptualising in order to meet the exciting and radical changes in schools that lie ahead over the next ten years.

Education reform, particularly in relation to *Every Child Matters* and the Full-Service Extended School, requires every teacher to make a difference for the better to every child's life by improving the outcomes for all children and young people, including the most disadvantaged. There is an increasing emphasis on schools adopting a more holistic approach towards meeting the needs of the 'whole' child.

Table 1.1 exemplifies the changing role of the classroom teacher, from the pre-*Every Child Matters* era to schools of the future, in the twenty-first century.

Table 1.1 Classroom teachers' changing role

OLD ROLE PRE-*EVERY CHILD MATTERS*	NEW ROLE FOR TWENTY-FIRST CENTURY
Within-child focus Deficit and medical model Child's difficulties are the main problem	Holistic whole-child approach *Every Child Matters* focus on the five outcomes for children's well-being
Withdrawal, segregated individual pupil and small-group direct teaching for those with more complex and challenging additional educational needs	In-class inclusive approach to meet a diversity of pupils with additional educational needs Quality First Teaching *Removing Barriers to Achievement*
Seeks specialist diagnostic assessment	Assessment for learning – pupil-friendly, e.g. P-scales, PIVATS, EAL scale, EBD scale Pupil self-review of progress
Specific individual pupil programmes with little or no transference across the curriculum	Personalised learning approaches, personalised learning and career pathways, and personalised services providing 'wrap around' care, tailored to meet the needs of the whole child

Teachers have an important role to play in shaping the provision and extended services that children and young people receive, both within the school and in the local community, beyond the formal school day. There will be an increasing need to challenge existing practice and the status quo, to move out of the 'comfort zone', and away from familiar ways of working.

In the White Paper *Higher Standards, Better Schools for All* the government comments:

> No longer will it be acceptable for young people to be denied the opportunity to achieve their full potential, whatever their abilities and talents; or for artificial barriers to prevent choice and diversity from playing its full part in delivering a good education for every child.
>
> (DfES 2005j: Summary)

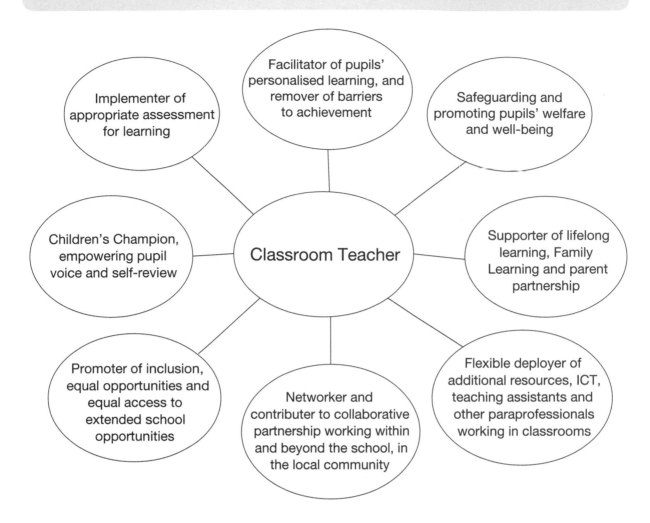

Figure 1.1 Classroom teachers' core role in twenty-first century schools

Educational settings for teachers in the twenty-first century

Teachers in the twenty-first century have a far greater choice of educational settings they can work in, and the government's Change for Children programme opens up many new and exciting opportunities.

Children's Centres

Sure Start Children's Centres, open from 8 a.m. to 6 p.m. all year round, provide seamless holistic personalised integrated services and information for children aged under 5 and their families. Help can also be accessed from multi-disciplinary teams of professionals. These centres are based on the concept that providing integrated education, childcare, family support and health services are key factors in determining good outcomes for children and their parents, and improving children's life chances.

Research has revealed that good quality pre-school education enhances intellectual development and improves independence, concentration and sociability in young children. Sure Start Children's Centres are a vital part of the government's Ten Year Strategy for Childcare, enabling all families with children to have access to an affordable, flexible, high quality childcare place for their child.

In 2008, there will be 1,700 Children's Centres in England, and by 2010 there will be a Sure Start Children's Centre in every community. Schools, and particularly extended schools, provide

Table 1.2 The government's programme of change

FIVE YEAR STRATEGY FOR CHILDREN AND LEARNERS

Children's Centres in or around school sites, one-stop shops open from 8 a.m. to 6 p.m. providing a range of services and outreach

Full-Service Extended Schools

Every School a Healthy School

Widening of primary curriculum – PE/sport, play music, learn a language

Networks of primary schools supporting and challenging each other

Building Schools for the Future – refurbished, rebuilt new secondary schools

Specialist Schools expanding, with some to have second specialisms, e.g. in SEN, and more **Academies**

Foundation Partnerships – schools with collective responsibilities for 14–19 curriculum, SEN, excluded pupils

KS3 Strategy to Secondary Strategy 11–16 from April 2005

New Relationship with Schools – self-evaluation and school improvement partner; **new School Profile**

Three Year Budgets for Schools

TEN YEAR STRATEGY FOR CHILDCARE (BIRTH TO 14)

Flexible, accessible, affordable high quality childcare

Sure Start Children's Centres in every community by 2010

15 hours per week for 38 weeks' free 'educare' for 3–4 year olds by 2010

Expanding maternity leave entitlement to 9 months' paid maternity leave from 2007, and **increase in childcare element of Working Tax Credit**

Childcare for 5–14-year-olds based in schools with affordable school-based childcare on weekdays for 5–11-year-olds between 8 a.m. and 6 p.m.

Secondary Schools open on weekdays by 2010 from 8 a.m. to 6 p.m. offering a range of activities – art, music, sport, ICT

All full-time daycare settings led by graduate qualified Early Years teachers

Introduction of a new legal framework for the regulation and inspection of early education and childcare services

Greater partnership working between LAs, childcare providers and **Children's Trusts**

14–19 STRATEGY

5 key proposals:

Participation – increased at 17 from 75% to 90% over next 10 years

Addressing disengagement – more choice of where to study, greater vocational opportunities and work-based learning, apprenticeships

Focusing on the basics 11–14 and 14–19 with reduced prescription, catch-up in English and Maths, stretch for all pupils, Pupil Profile at 14 recording achievement across the curriculum

Reform of vocational routes – introducing Diplomas in 14 occupational lines of learning, Diplomas in 3 levels: 1 (Foundation); 2 (GCSE); 3 (advanced). Increased number and quality of apprenticeships, work placements

Stretch, differentiation and challenge – GCSE and A levels retained but improved by reduced amount of assessment in GCSE coursework and from 6 to 4 assessments for each A-level; harder optional questions at A-level for most able, extended project, HE modules early

Removing Barriers to Achievement – The Government's Strategy for SEN

4 key areas:

Early intervention and help provided for children with learning difficulties, and accessible childcare for parents of children with SEN and disabilities

Removing barriers to learning by embedding inclusive practice in every school and Early Years setting; increasing opportunities and widening access to mainstream; sharing expertise between special and mainstream schools

Raising expectations and achievement by developing teachers' skills and strategies to meet needs of SEN by personalising learning, developing a flexible curriculum and by using appropriate smaller-stepped assessment for learning

Delivering improvements in partnership to provide 'wraparound' health and social care integrated services in and around schools.

Giving parents greater confidence in mainstream education for their child with SEN and disability

Every Child Matters

5 outcomes for children: being healthy, staying safe, enjoying and achieving, making a positive contribution, achieving social and economic well-being

Early intervention and effective provision

Improving information sharing between agencies to speed up the process of obtaining help and support needed for children and families

Developing a Common Assessment Framework across services

Introducing a named 'lead professional' to co-ordinate services for children to meet their needs

Developing wraparound care multi-disciplinary service delivery in and around schools and in Children's Centres

Safeguarding Children partnership arrangements

Common occupational standards for all agencies working with children (Workforce Reform)

Integrated inspection framework for Children's Services

Every Child Matters – Inspection Framework

Effectiveness and efficiency of current provision and related services in meeting the full range of learners' needs, and what requires further improvement

Achievement and standards

1. How well do learners achieve?

Quality of provision

2. How effective are teaching, training and learning?
3. How well do programmes and activities meet the needs and interests of learners?
4. How well are learners guided and supported?

Leadership and management

5. How effective are leadership and management in raising achievement and supporting all learners?

OFSTED judgements: (1 Outstanding; 2 Good; 3 Satisfactory; 4 Inadequate)

School self-evaluation and input from pupils, parents, stakeholders key, with focus on *Every Child Matters* 5 outcomes for children and young people excellent sites for the development of such a centre in a local area. Each Children's Centre will have a qualified Early Years teacher. There will be more opportunities for teachers from other settings to work within Children's Centres, e.g. Early Years teachers from special schools as well as mainstream primary schools, and Excellent Teachers and Leading Teachers for Early Years.

Sure Start Children's Centres in the most disadvantaged areas offer the following services:

- good quality learning combined with full daycare provision for children (minimum 10 hours a day, 5 days a week, 48 weeks a year);
- good quality teacher input to lead the development of learning within the centre;
- child and family health services, including ante-natal services;
- parental outreach;
- family support services;
- a base for a childminder network;
- support for children and parents with special needs;
- effective links with Jobcentre Plus to support parents/carers who wish to consider training or employment.

Sure Start Children's Centres in more advantaged areas offer a minimum range of services which includes:

- appropriate support and outreach services to parents/carers and children who have been identified as in need of such support and services;
- information and advice to parents/carers on a range of subjects, including local childcare, looking after babies and young children, local Early Years provision (childcare and early learning) education services for 3- and 4-year-olds;
- support for childminders;
- drop-in sessions and other activities for children and carers at the centre;
- links to Jobcentre Plus services.

Extended schools

There are two types of extended school in which teachers can work within the primary or secondary phase of education: the first is referred to as the Full-Service Extended School and the second is known as the Extended School.

The Full-Service Extended School differs from the Extended School in that it offers a more comprehensive range of co-located services provided by non-educational agencies such as health and social care on a single site. There are fewer Full-Service Extended Schools in local authority areas than Extended Schools. Full-Service Extended Schools are likely to employ a Full-Service Co-ordinator, who frees up head teachers and teachers to concentrate on their core business of teaching. Having key professionals such as health workers, psychologists and youth workers based on school sites and working closely alongside teachers means that children's problems can be addressed more effectively with less disruption to their learning.

Either type of extended school provides a range of services and activities often beyond the school day to help meet the needs of its pupils, their families and the wider community. While there is no blueprint for the types of activities extended schools might provide, schools can develop as little or as much additional provision to suit their own community needs. Local schools are able to cluster together to provide a wider range of services across several locations, with each school developing different activities and services. A school's extended services are designed to complement existing local provision.

By 2010, all children will be able to access through extended schools a core offer of extended services which includes:

- high quality 'wraparound' childcare provided by the school's site or through other local providers, available from 8 a.m. to 6 p.m. all year round;
- a varied menu of activities on offer such as homework clubs and study support, sport, music tuition, special interest clubs and volunteering;
- parenting support including information sessions for parents at key transition points, parenting programmes and family learning sessions;
- swift and easy referral to a wide range of specialist support services such as speech and language therapy, family support services and behaviour support;
- provision of wider community access to ICT, and sports and arts facilities, including adult learning.

Support from school staff to particular areas of the extended school's work is optional. However, certain community activities such as extra sports activities can become part of a teacher's core work. Such additional roles offer good opportunities for career development and flexible working hours.

The benefits of schools offering extended activities and services include:

- higher levels of pupil achievement, pupil motivation and self-esteem;
- specialist support to meet pupils' wider needs;
- additional facilities and equipment;
- enhanced partnership working with the community;
- easier access to essential services for staff.

Specialist schools

The Specialist Schools Programme, which began in 1994, is designed to help secondary schools, and, from 2005, maintained and non-maintained special schools, in partnership with private sector sponsors and additionally supported by government funding. The programme aims to establish distinctive identities through schools' chosen curricular specialisms, operating as curriculum centres of excellence, to promote school improvement and the raising of standards. While specialist schools have a special focus on those subjects relating to their chosen specialism, they must continue to meet the National Curriculum requirements and deliver a broad and balanced education to all pupils.

Secondary and special schools in England can apply for specialist status in one of ten curricular specialisms: arts, business and enterprise, engineering, humanities, languages, mathematics and computing, music, science, sports and technology. Schools can also combine any two specialisms. In 2005, the Specialist Schools Programme was further extended to enable maintained and non-maintained special schools to specialise in one of the four areas of the SEN Code of Practice: communication and interaction; cognition and learning; behavioural, emotional and social difficulties; and sensory and/or physical needs. SEN specialist school status fosters greater networking, partnership and outreach working for staff between special and mainstream secondary schools to meet the wider *Every Child Matters* outcomes for children. From 2004, high performing specialist schools that could demonstrate a greater level of additionality were able to take on extra roles by contributing to Training School Status and/or Leading Edge Status.

Academies

Academies are publicly funded independent schools that provide a first-class free education to pupils of all abilities usually aged 11–16 or 11–18. Some Academies provide education for pupils in both primary and secondary phases. Like maintained schools with a specialism, they may select up to 10 per cent of pupils on the basis of an aptitude for some specialisms. They are not governed by much of the education legislation, which applies to the maintained sector, apart from having regard to the SEN Code of Practice and to the Secretary of State's guidance on exclusions.

Academies are established by sponsors from business, faith or voluntary groups working with partners from the local community to replace one or more existing schools with low levels of performance, or where there is a need for a new school as part of the Building Schools for the Future initiative.

Academies make the fullest use of ICT; they provide a teaching and learning environment in line with the best in the maintained sector and offer a broad, relevant, innovative and balanced curriculum, focusing especially on one or more subject areas. As well as providing the best opportunities for the most able pupils and those needing additional support through curriculum enrichment and study support, Academies have a key role to play in the regeneration of communities. The independent status of Academies allows them the flexibility to be creative in their management, governance, teaching and curriculum, to find innovative solutions to meet local needs. They can help to support capacity building in other schools by disseminating their good practice and sharing their expertise. Academies are an important resource for the local family of schools, serving the local community in which they are established, including sharing their facilities with the community. They have greater freedom to tackle the local problems associated with poor or low pupil performance.

Academies are encouraged to take account of the National Agreement relating to tackling teacher workload. Teachers who choose to work in an Academy must have Qualified Teacher Status (QTS). Teachers and support staff working in Academies experience no barriers to a successful career which combines experience in both Academies and the maintained sector. The service in an Academy counts as qualifying service for teachers. While Academies, as independent schools, are not bound by the School Teachers' Pay and Conditions or by guidance on support staff pay and conditions issued by the National Joint Council for Local Government Services, they are able to negotiate pay and conditions arrangements for staff to meet the particular needs of the Academy and its pupils. Academies can make their own arrangements for rewarding excellent performance by teachers or support staff; for contribution to teaching in the Academy's specialism or in other specialist areas of the curriculum, and in recruiting staff in shortage subject areas.

Advanced Skills Teachers (ASTs) appointed to Academies are able to negotiate salary arrangements in line with those in place for ASTs. Any ASTs who transfer to a non-AST post in an Academy will have their salary arrangements protected for a period of time. Teachers working in Academies are able to access the AST and Excellent Teachers process at no extra cost to the Academy. Academies are able to appoint Fast Track, high calibre graduate teachers in the same way as schools. The careers of Academy teachers on the Fast Track Programme are supported centrally for up to five years.

Working in an Academy, a teacher can be expected to be involved in:

- using personalised learning approaches and modular learning paths with pupils;
- operating beyond the traditional school day in a fully accessible way to take learning beyond the Academy setting out into pupils' homes and the local community;

- using appropriate assessment for learning;
- offering personal tutor and peer mentoring systems for pupils;
- delivering extension programmes and accelerated learning opportunities using ICT and distance learning materials;
- using community champions;
- ensuring greater curriculum continuity partnerships with feeder schools;
- providing outreach and collaboration with neighbouring schools and other learning environments;
- innovating and doing things differently from maintained schools;
- following a programme of continuing professional development.

City Learning Centres

City Learning Centres (CLCs) are part of the Excellence in Cities (EiC) programme. The first CLCs opened in October 2000, and by March 2004 there were 105. City Learning Centres are located mainly on secondary school sites. They are a shared resource for the host school and all the other schools in the CLC partnership, although legal ownership usually lies with the local authority or the host school. CLCs have a management board, which includes representatives from some or all of the partnership schools, from local primary schools, and the wider community.

City Learning Centres provide 'state of the art' information and communication technology (ICT)-based enhanced teaching and learning opportunities across the curriculum for pupils and teachers within a network of local schools and in the wider community. They share facilities, develop resources, and plan and deliver alternative curriculum projects and activities with partner schools through the use of technology. CLCs acting as high technology centres of excellence with a range of facilities create stimulating, dynamic, exciting and challenging learning opportunities in subjects such as the creative arts, media, sports and healthy living. They promote community and lifelong learning opportunities and seek innovative ways to deliver teaching and learning.

Trust Schools

Every mainstream school can become a Trust School, and have a self-governing Trust, which is non-profit making, similar to that of an Academy. This enables schools to have the freedom to work with new partners such as businesses, charities, faith groups, to help develop their ethos and raise standards. They are able to employ their own staff, control their own assets and set their own admissions arrangements. Such schools can apply to the Secretary of State for Education for additional flexibilities, i.e. freedoms over pay and conditions for staff, and additional curriculum flexibilities.

Where Trust Schools have appointed the majority of the governing body comprising elected parents, staff governors and representatives from the local authority and the local community, they must establish a Parents' Council. This provides a forum whereby parents can have a strong voice in decisions about the way the school is run.

Trusts can be associated with more than one school, and this helps to drive innovation and best practice rapidly across a number of schools.

Collaborative working partnerships offering new challenges to teachers

Federations

The term 'federation' implies a degree of shared purpose, co-operation and a sense of accountability to each other and to the federation as a whole, while retaining a sense of local autonomy. The term federation describes many different types of collaborative groups, partnerships and clusters, school mergers and newly created schools. One key purpose for developing a federation of schools is to create a culture in which transformation is possible.

School federations, bringing together groups of schools, are viewed as offering significant potential to raise standards. Federations are able to drive school improvement across a group of schools, overcoming isolation and sharing good practice. A variety of federation models exists:

- a successful school brought together with a failing school;
- a group of schools with a joint governing body and a single Chief Executive;
- a federation of specialist schools serving an area, each playing to their strengths while increasing choice for all pupils.

Successful federations demonstrate a high commitment to the concept of a learning community, promoting inclusion, building capacity between schools coherently, finding new ways of approaching teaching and learning, and meeting stakeholders' expectations at both local and federal levels. They play a significant part in improving the life chances and well-being of all pupils. Federations have a number of benefits to teachers working together across a group of schools, e.g. sharing professional development, staff expertise, resources, curriculum developments, leadership and management. Joint staffing opportunities, including Specialist Teachers and wider career opportunities across the federation, are often available.

Networked Learning Communities

Networked Learning Communities were developed through the National College for School Leadership (NCSL). These are a loose federation of schools pursuing a common interest, through an agreed project plan, focused on school improvement. Networked Learning Communities do the following:

- design around a compelling idea or aspirational purpose;
- focus on pupil learning;
- create new opportunities for adult learning;
- plan and have dedicated leadership and management.

Schools working together in Networked Learning Communities add significantly to teachers' professional development by:

- broadening teacher expertise and learning opportunities available to pupils;
- providing a direct mechanism for sharing expert teacher practice, e.g. through collaborative coaching and mentoring, teacher exchanges and 'learning walks' (structured school-to-school visits);
- providing the diversity, flexibility and range of opportunities that no single school can offer;
- nurturing creativity, risk-taking and innovation among staff to improve learning and teaching;
- leading to improvement in pupils' attainment and well-being through teachers and other supporting adults doing things differently, or doing different things in classrooms;
- leading to improved teaching.

Collaboration within networks engages teachers and other staff in participating actively in developing their own practice and that of others. It creates a dynamic process of interpretation and evaluation of practice between colleagues, extending beyond the single classroom or school. Enquiry (the process of systematically exploring and considering research information from experts and practitioners in classrooms) helps teachers' decision-making and problem-solving. Collaborative enquiry between teachers promotes reflection, challenging individual and collective experiences in order to obtain a deepened understanding of shared beliefs and practices within the Networked Learning Community.

Leading Edge Partnership Programme

Leading Edge Partnerships enable teachers to work together to tackle identified challenges in the drive to raise standards. A lead school is given £60,000 a year for three years to use across their partnership of schools for an agreed programme of activities, working on locally determined learning challenges. Partnerships are committed to working collaboratively to inspire, design, test and adapt professional practice to raise standards of teaching and learning where improvement is most urgently needed.

There is a particular focus on partnering with schools struggling to raise standards, particularly in instances concerning underachieving groups of pupils from poorer socio-economic backgrounds and from particular minority ethnic groups.

There are 205 partnerships in the programme in England. High performing specialist schools, at re-designation, can take on leading roles in the Leading Edge Partnership Programme, as part of the government's Five Year Strategy for Children and Learners.

Partnerships have the opportunity nationally to showcase the work they have been doing and demonstrate the impact it has had at Innovative Exchange Events. The annual national showcase event demonstrates informed professionalism in practice, enabling teachers and senior managers from schools to share practices across the country as well as across their partnership. Teachers involved in the Leading Edge Partnership are able to make recommendations on programme development and policy via related sub-groups, which feed into a national steering group. Lead and partner schools evaluate their work, and the DfES disseminates the good practice on their Leading Edge website.

Education Improvement Partnerships

Education Improvement Partnerships (EIPs) as part of the government's Five Year Strategy for Children and Learners are designed to give some unity and sharper purpose to the idea of collaboration across schools in a local community. EIPs can make valuable contributions to 14–19 provision, behaviour improvement and alternative educational provision, and to the development of childcare and extended services. The objectives of EIPs are to:

- raise attainment, and improve behaviour and attendance in partnership schools;
- personalise provision for children and young people;
- deliver on the five *Every Child Matters* outcomes in all partnership schools through extended services;
- contribute to ongoing staff professional development.

While there is no limit to the number of schools in an EIP, between 5 and 30 schools in a partnership is recommended. The make-up of schools in the EIP is dependent on local needs. Benefits of EIPs for teachers include:

- increased staff motivation at all levels through professional dialogue with partner schools;
- positive solution focused approaches developed between staff to resolve local issues between schools;
- greater sharing of provision and responsibility for disruptive and excluded pupils across partnership schools;
- increased sharing of resources to meet the *Every Child Matters* agenda;
- sharing a broader curriculum provision, including a wider range of out-of-school activities.

Children's trusts

Children's trusts, underpinned by the Children Act 2004 duty to co-operate, bring together all services for children and young people in an area. All local authority areas will be expected to have a children's trust, or something similar, by 2008 that is organic, flexible and responsive to local circumstances and need. Children's trusts are partnerships between different organisations that provide, commission and deliver better outcomes for children and young people. Local authorities lead children's trusts strategically, with the director of children's services being accountable for the services provided by the trust, and the lead member of the Council being politically accountable. The local authority children's services department will facilitate, encourage and support schools in its area to contribute to, and benefit from, children's trust activity, and will ensure their views are sought and fed back.

Children's trust arrangements have four essential components:

1. professionals enabled and encouraged to work together in more integrated front-line services, built around the needs of children and young people;
2. common processes designed to create and underpin joint working;
3. a planning and commissioning framework which brings together agencies' planning, supported by pooled budgets and resources to ensure key priorities are identified and addressed;
4. strong inter-agency governance arrangements with shared ownership, clear accountability and clear terms of reference.

Children's trusts help to develop and establish new ways of working, a new learning culture and a coherent training programme for all key participants and partners across services and organisations. They support those who work every day with children and young people and their families, including teachers in schools, through closer working between school staff and other children's professionals from health, social services and voluntary organisations.

Schools have a strong role to play in local partnerships such as children's trusts. The new school profile, which is replacing the annual report to parents, gives schools the opportunity to set out clearly for parents the full range of services they offer. Schools will be able to feed their views into local service planning through children's trust involvement, as well as providing services as an individual school, or in partnership with a network of other schools.

Children's trusts provide an excellent opportunity for extended schools to strengthen and widen their remit of the extended services they provide. Extended schools may be commissioned by children's trusts to deliver integrated children's services co-located on the school site. Head teachers may be a member on the children's trust partnership board, and involved in developing the local commissioning strategy.

Challenges for teachers

New educational settings and increased collaborative partnership working across schools create exciting challenges for teachers as a result of:

- greater focus on the child and family through *Every Child Matters*;
- re-conceptualisation of professions, including teaching, through remodelling of the workforce;
- a commitment to personalisation in all government strategies that impact on schools' provision;
- an increased commitment to stakeholder empowerment, particularly of children, young people and their parents/carers;
- greater emphasis on understanding the interdependency of home, school and the community.

The government's White Paper *Higher Standards, Better Schools for All* identifies the three great challenges that must be addressed:

1 tailor education around the needs of each individual child – so that no child falls behind and no child is held back from achieving their potential;
2 put parents at the centre of our thinking – giving them greater choice and active engagement in their child's learning and how schools are run; and
3 empower schools and teachers to respond to local and parental demands, injecting dynamism and innovation into our schools.

(DfES 2005j: Foreword)

Every teacher has a duty to ensure that every child receives an excellent education, whatever their background and wherever they live.

2

Every Child Matters: Implications for Teachers

Every Child Matters: Change for Children programme in schools

The government's ambitions set out in *Every Child Matters* are aimed at improving the outcomes for all children and young people, including the most disadvantaged and those with additional needs, by intervening early to prevent things from going wrong in the first place. The philosophy behind the government's *Every Child Matters* Change for Children programme is to protect, nurture and improve the life chances of children and young people, in particular, the life chances of vulnerable children, including those in public care (LACs); children with learning difficulties and disabilities; travellers, asylum seekers and refugees; excluded pupils; truants; young offenders; family carers; children living in families where parents have mental illness, alcohol or drug dependency problems; and children affected by domestic violence.

The tragic death of Victoria Climbié prompted *Every Child Matters*. The issue in this particular case was not about the lack of resources from services, but about practitioners from multi-agencies needing to respond to key questions much earlier, e.g.:

- What is a day like in the life of this child?
- Why is this child never in school?
- What could the service have done to safeguard and improve the life chances of this vulnerable child at risk?

Facts about vulnerable children at risk:

- Between one and two children die every week in England and Wales as a result of abuse and neglect.
- 900,000 children live in families where there is a serious alcohol problem.
- Every day, up to 5,000 children attempt to ring the ChildLine helpline because they are being physically or sexually abused, have run away from home, or are homeless or suicidal, and some of those children are as young as five.
- Every day, on average, 81 children are taken into care, and 87 are added to child protection registers.
- One in ten children has mental health problems.

Every Child Matters: key messages for inclusive schools

> Raising standards in schools and inclusion go hand in hand. In particular schools have a critical role in raising the educational achievement of children in care, and other groups that have consistently underachieved.
>
> (DfES 2004f: 4.6)

- Children cannot learn effectively if they do not feel safe or if health problems create barriers to learning.
- Pupil performance and well-being go hand in hand.
- Every child to fulfil their potential.
- Personalisation as a principle must involve users (children and parents) in shaping and developing the delivery of education and related services in and around schools.
- Schools to adopt more of a multi-professional focus, no longer being the sole site and provider of learning.

The five outcomes for children and young people which are central to the programme of change are given legal force in the Children Act 2004, as the components of well-being with the purpose of promoting co-operation between agencies. The outcomes are interdependent and show the important relationship between educational achievement and well-being.

Schools as service providers to children and families

Schools already contribute to pupils' wider well-being by:

- helping each pupil achieve the highest educational standards they possibly can;
- dealing with bullying and discrimination, and keeping children safe;
- becoming Healthy Schools and promoting healthy lifestyles through Personal, Social and Health Education (PSHE) lessons, drugs education, breakfast clubs and sporting activities;
- ensuring attendance, encouraging pupils to behave responsibly, giving them a strong 'voice' in the life of the school and encouraging them to help others in school and in the community;
- helping communities to value education and be aware that it is the route out of the poverty trap;
- engaging and helping parents in actively supporting their children's learning and development.

Schools acting as 'hubs' for lifelong learning and personalised services for children, young people and families have an opportunity to extend their provision to meet the needs of their local community, and to get to know their client/consumer groups better. Schools providing services needed by local people become the focus of the local community and boost community pride and involvement.

One young person's view (Lisa, aged 16–18) in *Every Child Matters: Next Steps*, was:

> I like the idea of schools being more open and being used by the wider community. I think the youth and the rest of the community are separated and need to be more involved and know about what is going on. This applies to the community knowing about what the school is doing and the schools knowing about what is going on in the community.

(DfES 2004f: 8)

Every Child Matters considerably increases the responsibility and accountability of all teachers working in a range of educational settings. Everyone working in a school has a role to play in a local programme of change for children, which focuses on the needs of the 'whole' child, whether a head teacher, classroom teacher, teaching assistant (TA), Learning Mentor, governor, site manager, midday supervisor or a pupil.

Safeguarding children

Safeguarding children and young people and promoting their welfare is everyone's duty in a school. Revised guidance on safeguarding children was issued in 2004 to schools (DfES 2004n). Two aspects were identified in relation to safeguarding and promoting the welfare of children. These were:

1 arrangements to take all reasonable measures to ensure that risks of harm to children's welfare are minimised; and
2 arrangements to take all appropriate actions to address concerns about the welfare of a child, or children, working to agreed local policies and procedures in full partnership with other local agencies.

Safeguarding covers issues such as pupil health and safety and bullying, as well as arrangements for meeting the medical needs of children with medical conditions, providing first aid, school security, safeguarding against drugs and substance misuse.

All schools must have a designated trained senior member of staff to take lead responsibility for dealing with child protection issues, who provides advice and support to other staff in school. Child protection relates to where a child is suffering or is likely to suffer significant harm, i.e. ill treatment or the impairment of health and development, including impairment suffered from seeing or hearing the ill treatment of others. Ill treatment includes sexual abuse and all other forms of ill treatment which are not physical, e.g. emotional ill treatment, which involves conveying to children that they are worthless, unloved or inadequate.

The role of the designated teacher for child protection and safeguarding in school is to:

- know the correct child protection procedures, and keep their training up to date;
- ensure the correct child protection procedures are followed consistently in school;
- refer cases immediately to the appropriate service and then inform the head teacher;
- organise whole-school training for safeguarding and child protection;
- disseminate relevant training materials and advice to staff;
- have robust systems in place for child protection, documenting and recording referrals and disclosures;
- liaise regularly and speedily with agencies;
- represent the school at child protection meetings and case conferences;
- provide support to staff, particularly when a pupil makes a disclosure to a member of staff;
- monitor the school's child protection policy, procedures and outcomes.

All staff working with children in schools, including teachers, must update their child protection training every three years. Training in child protection and safeguarding must form part of the course of training leading to Qualified Teacher Status (QTS).

Staff in schools are often best placed to notice early signs of distress and symptoms of abuse existing among pupils. If a teacher or any member of staff in school has concerns about a child's welfare, or if a child discloses that he/she is suffering abuse, or reveals information that gives serious cause for concern, the member of staff should inform and refer the exact cause for concern or disclosure to the designated child protection officer in school, during the same working day. The member of staff making the referral should be given feedback on the outcome of the referral. When a child makes a disclosure to a member of staff in school, the teacher or supporting adult must be careful, apart from ascertaining basic facts, not to ask the child leading questions. The welfare of the child is always paramount; teachers have a duty to safeguard and promote the welfare of children, and must refer a child's disclosure. However, teachers must exercise care and sensitivity when sharing information, in order to respect confidentiality, without compromising the safety of the child.

According to guidance from the National Network of Investigation and Referral Support Co-ordinators (IRSC), teachers need to be aware that some factors may prevent children from disclosing:

- direct threats if the child talks to others;
- fear of punishment;
- guilt and shame;
- no-one listening;
- lack of trust;

- implications of telling, e.g. family break-up;
- not realising a situation is abusive.

Children and young people are more likely to feel able to make a disclosure to a teacher when:

- pupils' self-esteem is high;
- their views and contributions are respected;
- there is space for privacy in school;
- the school feels a safe place to be in;
- there is a culture of openness, honesty and trust;
- adults and children in school are respectful to each other;
- staff in school allow children to be heard without interruption.

Table 2.1 Change for Children

Key areas	Summary of Change for Children
Introduction	Change for Children was issued in December 2004. Four accompanying documents related specifically to schools, social care, criminal justice system and health services. It explained the national framework for local change programmes in order to build services around the needs of children and young people. It set out the action needed at local level in order to: ■ improve and integrate universal services in Early Years settings, schools and the health service; ■ provide more specialised help to act early and effectively to prevent and address problems; ■ reconfigure services around the child and family in one place, e.g. Children's Centre, extended schools, multi-disciplinary teams of professionals; ■ ensure dedicated and enterprising leadership at all levels of the system; ■ develop a shared sense of responsibility across agencies for safeguarding and protecting children from harm; ■ listen to children and young people and their families when assessing and planning service provision, and in direct delivery.
1. National framework for local change programmes	**The Children Act** (15 November 2004) established: ■ a Children's Commissioner to champion the views and interests of children and young people; ■ a duty on local authorities (LAs) to make arrangements to promote co-operation between agencies and other appropriate bodies (such as voluntary and community organisations) in order to improve children's well-being in relation to the five outcomes for children in *Every Child Matters*, and a duty on key partners to participate in the co-operation arrangements; ■ a duty on key agencies to safeguard and promote the welfare of children; ■ a duty on LAs to set up Local Safeguarding Children Boards and on key partners to take part; ■ provision for indexes or databases containing basic information about children and young people to enable better sharing of information; ■ a requirement for a single Children and Young People's Plan to be drawn up by each LA; ■ a requirement on LAs to appoint a Director of Children's Services and designate a Lead Member; ■ the creation of an integrated inspection framework and the conduct of Joint Area Reviews to assess local areas' progress in improving outcomes; ■ provisions relating to foster care, private fostering and the education of children in care. The National Service Framework for Children, Young People and Maternity Services (NSF) is integral to the implementation of the Children Act 2004, and local change programmes. Local change programmes will be stronger if set within a supportive national framework comprising key elements: policies and products, improvement cycle, supporting change, inspection criteria, targets and indicators, outcomes and aims.

Table 2.1 *(Continued)*

Key areas	Summary of Change for Children
2. Working towards better outcomes for children and young people	Five outcomes for children are central to the change programme; they are interdependent, and show important relationships between educational achievement and well-being. The **Outcomes Framework** will enable LAs with their partners to carry out a thorough needs analysis as a starting point for planning a local change programme. The results of the needs analysis will allow LAs and their partners to establish and agree their vision to improve outcomes for children and young people, to set priorities for action and to agree local targets. The Outcomes Framework will enable local children's services to be held accountable for delivering improved outcomes through integrated inspections using common criteria, developed with reference to the National Service Framework (NSF).
3. Integrated services and local change	Securing a shift from intervention to prevention, and meeting the needs of the most vulnerable. This re-shaping requires personalised and high quality, integrated universal services, which give easy access to effective and targeted specialist services, which will be delivered by a skilled and effective workforce, and utilise joint commissioning and pooled budgets.
4. Support for local change	Regional Change Advisers based in government offices supporting local areas in planning and implementing the local change programme; training for elected members in LAs; disseminating good practice on Children's Trusts; performance review, monitoring and assessment through integrated inspection of children's services; additional funding to LAs to support the Change for Children programme.

Table 2.2 Implications of *Every Child Matters* for teachers' role

Every Child Matters aspect	New role for teachers
Early intervention and effective protection	**Advocate and champion for pupils** – prompt referral to INCO/SENCO following data analysis and evidence gathering, of any pupils who have poor *Every Child Matters* outcomes that give cause for concern; safeguarding and promoting the welfare of pupils; promoting equal opportunities, inclusion, and equal access to extended school out-of-hours learning activities; empowering pupil 'voice', listening to pupils' views and acting on these promptly; enabling pupils to self-review their progress and effectiveness of additional provision.
Supporting parents and carers	**Parent partnership supporter** – promoting lifelong learning and Family Learning activities and opportunities; keeping parents/carers informed about their child's progress, achievements, well-being; providing practical strategies to parents/carers on how they can support their child's learning and well-being at home.
Multi-disciplinary teams of paraprofessionals	**Collaborative partner deploying additional resources effectively** – mobilising a range of resources within the classroom, e.g. teaching assistants, bilingual assistants, behaviour support teacher, speech and language therapist, ICT and multimedia technology, to respond to the needs of pupils with additional needs in order to improve their learning, behaviour, personal and social development and well-being, to remove barriers to learning and participation; clarify roles of paraprofessionals and the teacher working in partnership.
Integrated inspections of children's services (aligned to the *Every Child Matters* outcomes)	**Quality Assurance** – monitoring and evaluating pupil progress and well-being against the five *Every Child Matters* outcomes; tracking pupils' progress and analysing data to identify rates of pupils' progress in relation to their prior attainment; evaluating the impact of ICT, additional interventions and provision on pupils' outcomes (attainment, achievement and well-being).
Personalisation in learning, care and support	**Facilitator of personalised learning and care** – pupils being taught in an emotionally literate environment; working in partnership with paraprofessionals to minimise and remove barriers to learning and participation in order to make the curriculum and out-of-hours learning activities fully accessible to a diversity of learners; providing pupils with quality opportunities for personal, social and emotional development, helping them to manage their behaviour and well-being.

Table 2.3 Five outcomes for children and young people

Outcome	ECM aims/descriptor	OFSTED evidence descriptor
Being healthy	Physically, mentally and emotionally healthy; adopt healthy lifestyles; choose not to take illegal drugs; parents/carers, families promote healthy choices	Take regular exercise, including at least 2 hours' PE and sport a week; know about and make healthy lifestyle choices; understand sexual health risks and the dangers of smoking and substance abuse; eat and drink healthily; recognise the signs of personal stress and develop strategies to manage it
Staying safe	Safe from maltreatment, neglect, violence, sexual exploitation; safe from accidental injury and death; safe from bullying and discrimination; safe from crime and anti-social behaviour in and out of school; have security, stability and are cared for; parents/carers, families provide safe homes and stability	Display concern for others and refrain from intimidating and anti-social behaviour; feel safe from bullying and discrimination; feel confident to report bullying and racist incidents; act responsibly in high risk situations
Enjoying and achieving	Ready for school; attend and enjoy school; achieve stretching national educational standards in primary and secondary school; achieve personal and social development and enjoy recreation; parents/carers, families support learning	Have positive attitudes to education, behave well and have a good school attendance record
Making a positive contribution	Engage in decision-making and support the community and environment; engage in law-abiding and positive behaviour in and out of school; develop positive relationships and choose not to bully and discriminate; develop self-confidence and successfully deal with significant life changes and challenges; develop enterprising behaviour; parents/carers, families promote positive behaviour	Understand their legal and civil rights and responsibilities; show social responsibility, and refrain from bullying and discrimination; express their views at school and are confident their views and 'voice' will be heard; initiate and manage a range of organised activities in school and community organisations
Achieving economic and social well-being	Engage in further education, employment or training on leaving school; ready for employment; live in decent homes and sustainable communities; access to transport and material goods; live in households free from low income; parents/carers, families are supported to be economically active	Develop basic skills in literacy, numeracy and ICT; develop their self-confidence and team working skills; become enterprising, able to handle change, take initiative and calculate risk when making decisions; become financially literate and gain an understanding of business and the economy and of their career options; develop knowledge and skills when they are older, related to workplace situations

Model *Every Child Matters* School Policy Statement

(The following model statement can be adapted for inclusion in subject and whole-school policies.)

Every pupil with additional needs in this inclusive school has an entitlement to fulfil his/her optimum potential. This is achieved by ensuring the well-being of all pupils in relation to: being healthy, staying safe, enjoying and achieving, making a positive contribution, and achieving social and economic well-being.

These well-being outcomes are embraced in every aspect of school life: personalised teaching and learning approaches; access to ICT across the curriculum; flexible learning pathways and out-of-hours learning activities; support for emotional well-being; flexible timetables; assessment for learning which engages pupils in having a say about their progress and additional provision; and partnership with parents/carers, other schools, the local community and with practitioners from health, education and social services providing 'wrap around' care and personalised services.

Table 2.4 Examples of school activities linked to the *Every Child Matters* outcomes

Every Child Matters outcome	Example of school activities
Being healthy	Stress management programme for pupils and staff, which entails aromatherapy, relaxation techniques in a peaceful multi-sensory room within school.
Staying safe	Peer mediation introduced as a strategy to reduce incidents of bullying and discrimination among pupils.
Enjoying and achieving	Pupils with more complex learning difficulties and disabilities follow appropriate learning pathways across a range of educational settings and by a variety of learning approaches, e.g. distance learning, e-learning.
Making a positive contribution	Pupils with additional needs are involved in school projects and initiatives that engage them in 'real' activities that help others, e.g. peer mentoring, 'Befriending' scheme.
Achieving economic and social well-being	Pupils with additional needs are engaged in mini-enterprise projects which help to develop their financial literacy skills, team working skills, build their self-confidence and develop their problem-solving skills.

The 'voice' of the child and young person

Every Child Matters supports the adjustment of school systems to respond to the views of children and young people. Consulting with children and young people is at the heart of all multi-agency planning for the delivery of 'wrap around' care on or around school sites. The United Nations Convention on the Rights of the Child, Article 12 states:

> Children and young people have a right to be heard and play a part in the decisions that affect them.

Participation by pupils is a key element in informing and shaping the delivery of learning and personalised services to meet their needs. Pupil participation is open to all, no matter what their race, religion, gender or disability. Pupil participation is empowering; it helps to raise self-esteem, develop emotional growth and self-awareness, and promotes self-efficacy. Empowerment in learning refers to pupils reaching a stage where they feel confident to offer ideas, do things independently, and evaluate their own learning, rather than wait to be told what to do by an adult. Children need to be involved in decision-making about learning, additional provision and extended services because if they are not, they will only receive what adults think they want.

Teachers need to ensure pupils feel valued and important when communicating meaningfully with a diversity of children and young people. Involving pupils in decisions about their learning and additional provision helps to prepare them for making important choices later in life when they leave school. It also helps to reduce staff–pupil conflict. The teacher's role is to act as an empathetic guide and advocate for the child, equipping him/her with the necessary skills to

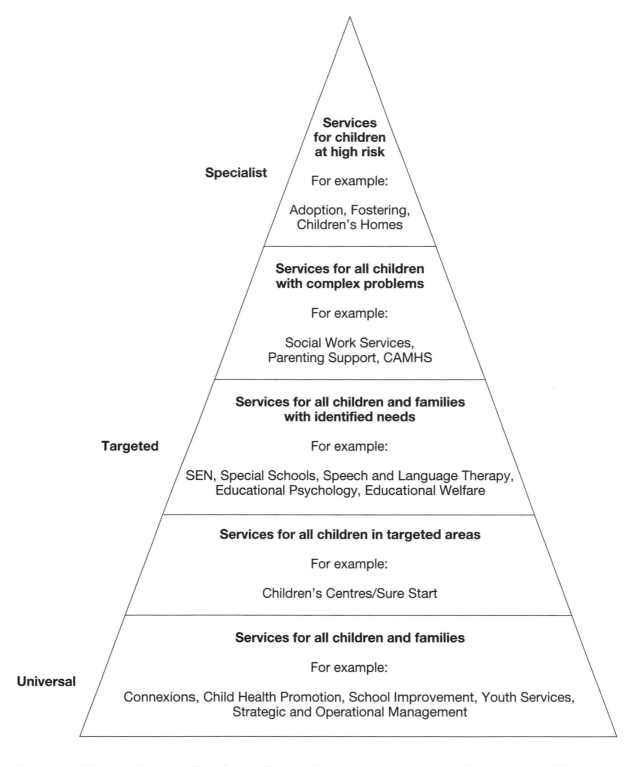

Figure 2.1 Universal, targeted and specialist services in and around schools. Source: DfES (2003b) *Every Child Matters*. London: Department for Education and Skills, p. 21.

respect different opinions and diverse cultures, i.e. learning how to negotiate with others, and to make compromises.

Teachers need to remember that children and young people are entitled to:

- have ownership of their learning;
- understand the learning and well-being process;
- experience a range of learning approaches and the application of multiple intelligences;

- develop their own tools for learning and well-being;
- express their feelings, value judgements and emotional needs through emotional literacy.

Teachers can empower individual learners by enabling them to identify:

- what their strengths and talents are;
- what their needs are;
- what their dreams and aspirations are;
- what they personally need to do to achieve their aspirations and goals;
- who can help them achieve their goals and aspirations;
- what help, resources, actions they need to reach and attain their goals.

Teachers may find the following questions useful to reflect upon in relation to *Every Child Matters* outcomes for children and young people.

- Are pupils safe in this school?
- Is this school a healthy school for pupils?
- Does this school make learning and achieving enjoyable for its pupils?
- Do pupils have the opportunity to make a positive contribution to the school and the wider community?
- Are pupils well prepared for the world of work and life outside and beyond school?
- How good are the *Every Child Matters* five outcomes in this school for pupils?
- Are the *Every Child Matters* five outcomes good enough for pupils in the school?
- What can teachers do to ensure that the *Every Child Matters* five outcomes for children are part of their everyday inclusive classroom practice?

CSIE (2002) found that pupils identify their ideal *Every Child Matters* inclusive school as being one that:

- values all pupils' different personalities and gifts, has no league tables, and does not compete with other schools;
- is safe, with swipe cards for the school gate; has anti-bullying alarms, first aid classes and a key person for pupils to talk to about problems;
- is respectful, treats pupils as individuals, enables children and adults to talk freely to each other, and values pupils' opinions;
- is flexible, without rigid timetables or exams or compulsory homework, and has no 'one-size-fits-all' curriculum.

Children and young people's rights

Schools and other settings such as Children's Centres do everything they can to ensure that learning and schooling is a positive experience for all children and young people.

The United Nations Convention on the Rights of the Child, Article 28 stipulates that:

- every child has the right to a free education;
- different kinds of education should be available for those with special needs;
- children have the right to be educated without fear;
- schools should have a bullying policy and each pupil should be informed of what to do if they find themselves being bullied.

Children's Commissioner

The Children's Commissioner was appointed in March 2005, and became fully operatio
1 July 2005. The Children's Commissioner acts as a national, independent voice for child.
young people. The Children's Commissioner's function is to promote awareness of views, n.
rights and interests of children and young people, so as to raise their profile and improve their
lives and well-being. This includes encouraging people working with children and with
responsibility for children, in the public and private sectors, to take account of children's and
young people's views and interests. The Commissioner has regard to the United Nations
Convention on the Rights of the Child when determining what constitutes the interests of
children and young people.

The Children's Commissioner is committed to four fundamental underpinning principles:
openness, honesty, transparency, and ownership. The Commissioner wants to see a society where:

- children and young people are valued, are expected to make a contribution to society and are
  supported in doing so;
- children and young people are truly at the centre of policy and practice;
- children and young people's views are actively sought, listened to and acted upon;
- children and young people's rights are upheld.

The Children's Commissioner aims to:

- promote the views, needs and interests of children and young people;
- make sure that children and young people are asked about their views and needs, have them
  listened to, and are taken seriously in society, and by agencies responsible for their welfare;
- promote the rights of children and young people;
- celebrate and generate discussion about the place of children and young people in society;
- build effective relationships with key people and organisations;
- research issues that matter to children and young people, particularly those which no-one else
  is dealing with;
- advocate, influence, scrutinise, challenge and pressurise for and on behalf of children and
  young people;
- be independent, yet develop effective collaboration, partnerships and alliances with others;
- be pioneering, creative and innovative.

The Children's Commissioner's website is www.childrenscommissioner.org

The Common Assessment process: pre-assessment checklist

A pre-assessment checklist forms part of the Common Assessment process. It acts as an early
identifier of children who would benefit from a Common Assessment, particularly for those who
may be at risk, or cause concern about their lack of progress in achieving all or any of the *Every
Child Matters* five outcomes. The pre-assessment checklist can be utilised by a range of multi-
agency practitioners, including class teachers. While it complements the Foundation Stage Profile,
the pre-assessment checklist can be used at any time during a child's journey through school.

The key question that a teacher must answer when considering whether it is appropriate to use
the pre-assessment checklist should be:

Is this child doing OK against the *Every Child Matters* five outcomes?

If a response of No is indicated for all or any of the five *Every Child Matters* outcomes on the pre-assessment checklist, then it will be necessary to undertake a Common Assessment. In a school, it will not necessarily be a teacher who undertakes the Common Assessment. However, teachers who work regularly with the child concerned are likely to be requested to make contributions to the Common Assessment evidence gathering process, along with other multi-agency professionals.

Table 2.5 Pre-assessment checklist

Does the child or young person appear to be:	Yes	No	Not sure	Evidence/Comment
healthy				
safe from harm				
learning and developing				
having a positive impact on others				
free from negative impact of poverty				

Source: DfES (2005b) *Common Assessment Framework for Children and Young People: Guide for service managers and practitioners.* London: Department for Education and Skills.

Common Assessment Framework

The Common Assessment Framework (CAF) helps schools to identify early when a pupil's needs can be met within the school and to enable better targeted referral to other specialist services. Common Assessment supports earlier intervention, improved multi-agency co-ordinated working, and helps teachers meet the wider needs of children and young people. The Common Assessment Framework process helps all practitioners from services (health, social services and education) to identify the broader needs of a child by using a national common and consistent approach to needs assessment for speedy referrals between agencies, in order to reduce the number of separate assessments for a child.

The Common Assessment is completed for children at risk of poor *Every Child Matters* outcomes where there are concerns about their lack of progress in learning; their health, welfare, behaviour or any other aspect of their well-being; and who require support from other agencies. Situations leading to a Common Assessment include those where a practitioner from health, social services and/or education has observed a significant change or a worrying feature in a child's appearance, demeanour or behaviour; or where a significant event in the child's life occurs; or where there are worries about the parents, carers or home, e.g. domestic violence, mental health issues, parental substance abuse/misuse, that might impact adversely on the child.

Situations where a Common Assessment might be initiated include children:

- missing developmental milestones or making slower progress than expected at school;
- presenting challenging or aggressive behaviours (e.g. bringing a knife into school), abusing/misusing substances or committing offences;
- experiencing physical or mental ill health or disability (either their own or their parents');
- being exposed to substance abuse/misuse, violence or crime within the family;
- undertaking caring responsibilities;
- experiencing bereavement or family breakdown;
- being bullied or are bullies themselves;
- being disadvantaged for reasons such as race, gender and disability;
- experiencing homelessness;
- being teenage parents or the child of teenage parents.

The list is not exhaustive. The presence of one or more of these elements does not in itself mean that the child has additional needs.

The Common Assessment can be undertaken at any time in a child's life from birth to 19. It is usually completed by front-line service workers in health, social services and education. Teachers working in a range of educational settings may be required to contribute relevant information to the Common Assessment process. It provides holistic information which augments decision-making at Action and Action Plus on the SEN Code of Practice graduated response for children with learning difficulties and disabilities (SEN). Information from the Common Assessment assists in informing the provision of relevant services to meet the child's needs.

The parents and carers of the child, as well as the child him/herself, where appropriate, must be consulted on the decision to undertake a Common Assessment. A copy of the assessment is provided to parents and carers to show to other services, in order to prevent repetition of information and reduce bureaucracy. Parents' refusal to complete a Common Assessment is recorded on the form. If a child is at serious risk of harm or vulnerable, the parents' failure to complete the assessment would not result in any delay in safeguarding the child, or in not taking prompt and early action by relevant service professionals.

Information sharing (IS) index

The information sharing (IS) index aids more effective prevention and early intervention and is a key element of the *Every Child Matters* programme. The IS index supports the delivery of other elements of the *Every Child Matters* programme, in particular, integrated processes such as the Common Assessment framework and lead professional, integrated front-line delivery including Children's Centres and extended schools. It helps to identify children missing education.

The IS index reduces the time taken by practitioners to find out which other services are involved with a child. The IS index enables practitioners delivering services to children to identify and contact one another more easily and quickly, so they can share relevant information about children who need services, or about whose welfare they are concerned. The index for information sharing encourages better communication between practitioners by indicating that there is information to share, that an assessment has occurred and/or that action has been taken.

Authorised practitioners in children's services, including education, health, social care, youth offending and some non-statutory voluntary services, can have access to the index. Access is granted according to the role of the practitioner, and may in many cases be through one or more central users, e.g. a teacher responsible for pastoral care or child protection (CP), rather than all teachers in a school.

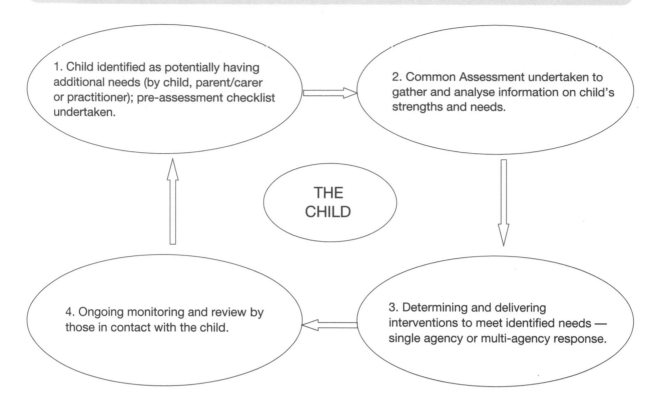

Figure 2.2 Cycle for effective case working in the Common Assessment Framework process. Source: DfES (2005b) *Common Assessment Framework for Children and Young People: Guide for Service Managers and Practitioners.*

Table 2.6 The Common Assessment Framework aspects and themes

Child development aspect	Parents and carers' aspect	Family and environmental aspect
General health, physical development, speech, language and communication development	Basic care – ensuring safety and protection	Family history – functioning and well-being
Employment and education – learning: understanding, reasoning and problem-solving; participation in learning; achievement and aspirations	Emotional warmth and stability	Employment – patterns and changes
Emotional, social and behavioural development	Guidance and boundaries – to enable the child to regulate own emotions and behaviour	Housing – quality, living arrangements
Identity – self-esteem, self-image, social presentation	Stimulation and encouragement to promote learning, intellectual development; promote social opportunities	Wider family – relationships with relatives and non-relatives
Family and social relationships		Family social integration
Self-care skills and independence		Social and community resources, including education (neighbourhood – impact, facilities and services)
		Income – financial considerations

Information held on the IS index is a record of all children from birth to 18 in England, and includes the following:

- name, address, gender and date of birth;
- an identifying number based on the existing Child Reference number/National Insurance number;
- name and contact details for:
  - parents or carers;
  - educational setting;
  - the primary medical practitioner (GP);
  - practitioners providing other services;
  - a lead professional for the child.

No assessment or case information is held on the IS index. All practitioners accessing the index must be CRB checked. The IS index will be fully implemented across all 150 local authorities in England by the end of 2008.

The National Service Framework for Children, Young People and Maternity Services

The National Service Framework (NSF) is integral to the implementation of the Children Act 2004 and local change programmes. It comprises 11 quality standards for health, social care and some education services, to be implemented over the next ten years for children and young people under 19.

The first five standards are universal and for all children and young people. The next five standards (Ss 6 to 10) cover services for children and young people requiring more specialised care, treatment and support. The final standard (S11) is for pregnant women and their partners.

The NSF aims to ensure high quality and integrated health and social care from pregnancy through to adulthood. The standards ensure that services and personalised care are designed and delivered around the needs of the child. They support a holistic child-centred approach, whereby not only the illness or the problem are looked at, but also the best ways to pick up problems early, take preventative action and ensure children have the best possible chance to realise their full potential are considered.

The NSF standards ensure that services for children, young people and their families in and around school communities are:

- quicker and easier to use and access;
- better at giving children, young people and their parents/carers increased information, power and choice over their care;
- more closely matched to individual and young people's needs;
- better co-ordinated so that the child does not see too many professionals;
- better at achieving good results for children and young people;
- better at involving children, young people and families in decisions about their care and well-being;
- closer to what children and young people say they want;
- able to safeguard and promote the welfare of children and young people.

Teachers will find NSF standards 5, 8, 9 and 10 have greater relevance to school settings, and to their role. The evidence-based NSF standards feed into the school self-evaluation process, indicating how the school's additional provision and extended services have impacted upon and improved the *Every Child Matters* five outcomes for children and young people's well-being, as well as their attainment.

The NSF standards support inclusion, and teachers must be aware of the impact and effectiveness that additional supporting adults, from within the school and from external agencies, have had on removing barriers to learning and on participation for the children and young people with additional needs.

The NSF service standards are summarised in Table 2.7.

Table 2.7 At-a-glance summary of the National Service Framework standards for children, young people and maternity services

Standard title	Standard descriptor	Main themes in standard
1. Promoting health and well-being, identifying needs and intervening early	The health and well-being of all children and young people is promoted and delivered through a co-ordinated programme of action, including prevention and early intervention wherever possible, to ensure long-term gain led by the NHS in partnership with local authorities.	Child Health Programme to reduce health inequalities. Multi-agency health promotion. Healthy lifestyles promoted. Universal and targeted health promotion. Access to targeted services. Early intervention and assessing needs.
2. Supporting parenting	Parents and carers are enabled to receive the information, services and support which will help them to care for their children and equip them with the skills they need to ensure that their children have optimum life chances and are healthy and safe.	Universal, targeted and specialist services to support mothers and fathers. Up-to-date information and education for parents. Support for parents of pre-school children to help children develop secure attachments and to develop. Support for parents of school-aged children to involve them in their child's learning and behaviour management. Early, multi-agency support for parents with specific needs, i.e. mental health problems, addiction to drugs, alcohol; parents of disabled children, teenage parents. Co-ordinated services across child and adult services. Multi-disciplinary support to meet the needs of adoptive parents/adults caring for looked after children.
3. Child, young person and family-centred services	Children and young people and families receive high quality services which are co-ordinated around their individual and family needs and take account of their views.	Appropriate information to children, young people and their parents. Listening and responding to them in relation to their care and treatment. Services respectful to the wishes of children and young people. Improved access to services. Robust multi-agency planning and commissioning arrangements, i.e. Children's Trusts, Common Assessment Framework.

Table 2.7 (*Continued*)

Standard title	Standard descriptor	Main themes in standard
		Quality and safety of care in delivering of child-centred services. Common core of skills, knowledge and competences for staff working with children and young people, across all agencies.
4. Growing up into adulthood	All young people have access to age-appropriate services which are responsive to their specific needs as they grow into adulthood.	Confidentiality and consent for young people. Health promotion to meet needs, i.e. reduce teenage pregnancy, smoking, substance misuse, suicide, sexually transmitted infections. Support achievement of full potential, e.g. Connexions and Youth Services. Improved access to services and advice for those who are disabled, in special circumstances or who live in rural areas. Transition to full adult services. Additional support available for looked after children leaving care and other young people in special circumstances.
5. Safeguarding and promoting the welfare of children and young people	All agencies work to prevent children suffering harm and to promote their welfare, provide them with the services they require to address their identified needs and safeguard children who are being or who are likely to be harmed.	All agencies prioritise safeguarding and promoting the welfare of children. LA Children and Young People's Plan. Clarification of agencies' roles and responsibilities. Profile of local population to identify and assess vulnerable children. High quality integrated services to meet needs of children at risk of harm, abused or neglected. Effective supervision for staff working with children to ensure clear, accurate, comprehensive, up-to-date records are kept, and high quality services delivered.
6. Children and young people who are ill	All children and young people who are ill or thought to be ill or injured will have timely access to appropriate advice and to effective services which address their health, social, educational and emotional needs throughout the period of their illness.	Comprehensive, integrated, timely local services. Professionals support children, young people and their families in self-care of their illness. Access to advice and services in a range of settings. Trained, competent professionals providing consistent advice to assist and treat a child who is ill. High quality treatment, and high quality care for those with long-term conditions. Prevention, assessment and treatment of pain management improved. Integrated Children's Community teams and Community Children's nursing services working outside hospital.

Table 2.7 (*Continued*)

Standard title	Standard descriptor	Main themes in standard
7. **Children and young people in hospital**	Children and young people receive high quality, evidence-based hospital care, developed through clinical governance and delivered in appropriate settings.	Care integrated and co-ordinated around their needs. Play for children in hospital is essential. Children, young people and their families treated with respect, involved in decision-making about their care, and given choices. Planned discharge from hospital for children. Hospital stay kept to a minimum. High quality evidence-based care provided. Hospitals meet responsibilities to safeguard and promote welfare of children. Care is provided in an appropriate location and in a safe environment.
8. **Disabled children and young people and those with complex health needs**	Children and young people who are disabled or who have complex health needs receive co-ordinated, high quality child- and family-centred services which are based on assessed needs, which promote social inclusion and, where possible, enable them and their families to live ordinary lives.	Services promote social inclusion. Increased access to hospital and primary health care services, therapy and equipment services, and social services. Early identification of health conditions, impairments and physical barriers to inclusion through integrated diagnosis and assessment processes. Early intervention and support to parents. Palliative care is available where needed. Services have robust systems to safeguard disabled children and young people. Multi-agency transition planning occurs to support adulthood.
9. **The mental health and psychological well-being of children and young people**	All children and young people, from birth to their eighteenth birthday, who have mental health problems and disorders have access to timely, integrated, high quality multi-disciplinary mental health services to ensure effective assessment, treatment and support, for them and their families.	Professional support for children's mental health is available in the Early Years. Staff working with children and young people contribute to early intervention and mental health promotion and develop good partnerships with children. Improved access to CAMHS with high quality multi-disciplinary CAMHS teams working in a range of settings. Gaps in service addressed particularly for those with learning disabilities. Care Networks developed and care in appropriate and safe settings.

Table 2.7 *(Continued)*

Standard title	Standard descriptor	Main themes in standard
10. Medicines for children and young people	Children, young people, their parents or carers, and health care professionals in all settings make decisions about medicines based on sound information about risk and benefit. They have access to safe and effective medicines that are prescribed on the basis of the best available evidence.	Safe medication practice. Use of unlicensed and off-label medicines comply with local and safety standards. Enhanced decision support for prescribers. Improved access to medicines. Clear, understandable, up-to-date information provided on medicines to users and parents. Greater support for those taking medication at home, in care and in education settings – safe storage, supply and administration of medicines. Equitable access to medicines and to safeguard children in special circumstances, disabled children and those with mental health disorders. Pharmacists' expertise is fully utilised.
11. Maternity services	Women have easy access to supportive, high quality maternity services, designed around their individual needs and those of their babies.	Women-centred care with easy access to information and support. Care pathways and managed care networks. Improved pre-conception care and access to a midwife as first point of contact. Local perinatal psychiatric services available. Choice of where best to give birth, i.e. home or maternity unit. Post-birth care provided based on a structured assessment. Breast-feeding information and support for mothers

Further activities for teachers related to *Every Child Matters*

The questions below, on aspects covered in this chapter related to *Every Child Matters*, will enable you as a teacher to discuss and identify ways forward in meeting the requirements of your changing role in the context of the national and local Change for Children programme.

- What progress have you already made as a teacher in starting to address and respond to the five outcomes of *Every Child Matters*?
- What barriers currently exist in your school that are likely to prevent you from fully implementing the *Every Child Matters* five outcomes for children and young people in your classroom?
- What action and next steps do you need to take in order to ensure that you implement the *Every Child Matters* five outcomes?
- Who else will you need to work with, from both within and outside school, to support you in applying and meeting the *Every Child Matters* five outcomes for children and young people?
- How do you intend to monitor and evaluate the *Every Child Matters* five outcomes in your classroom?

Removing Barriers to Achievement: Meeting a Diversity of Learners' Needs

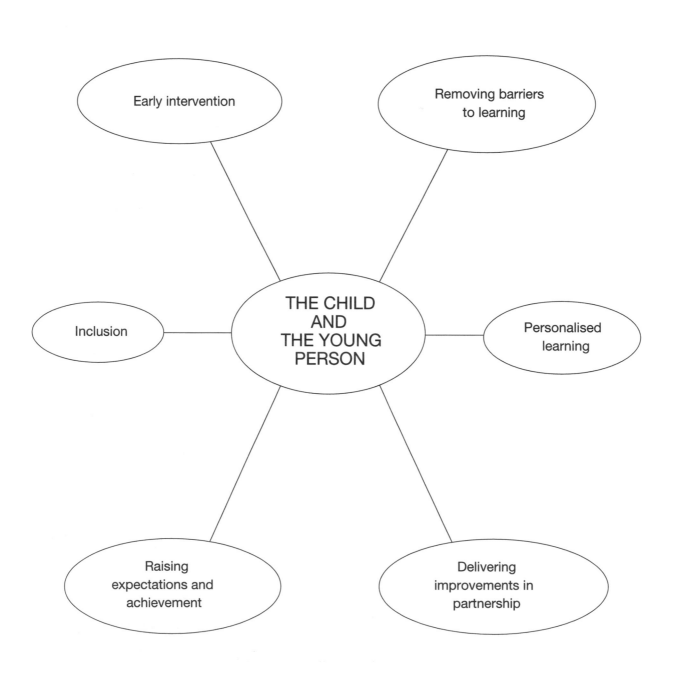

Table 3.1 *Removing Barriers to Achievement*: The government's strategy for SEN

Key area	Main features	Teacher role
Early intervention	Supporting early intervention; Improved information sharing between agencies; Skills and resources to take prompt action to help children falling behind peers; Provision of good quality, accessible childcare and Early Years provision; Delegation of SEN funding to schools to support early intervention; Better use of ICT to enable more time to be spent with SEN pupils; Raising the skills and awareness of staff to meet the needs of SEN pupils.	**Action researcher and solution assembler** to support early identification of SEN; **Communicator** sharing and filtering relevant information from agencies to staff, parents, pupils while respecting confidentiality and data and information sharing protocols; **Facilitator of personalised learning** to meet pupils' individual needs; **Leading Teacher** in SEN and inclusion.
Removing barriers to learning	Greater confidence to innovate; Skills and specialist support to meet SEN pupils' needs; Special and mainstream schools sharing skills and knowledge to support inclusion; Parents confident that their child's needs are met; Improved access for disabled pupils; Leadership in schools promotes inclusive practice; Residential provision reduced in special schools; Developing local communities of schools for local children; Access to study support, out-of-hours learning activities and care; Widening opportunities within the mainstream to include special school SEN pupils.	**Implementer** of RBA and ECM; **Collaborative partner** with the paraprofessional team; **Networker** sharing expertise, skills, knowledge with colleagues in other schools; **Mediator** maintaining positive relationships between parents, staff and SEN pupils; **Access provider** ensuring adaptations for disabled pupils to ensure access to curriculum, out-of-hours learning, written information and physical access to remove barriers to learning and participation; **Inclusion advocate** promoting emotional intelligence, empowering SEN pupils; creating an ethos of tolerance and acceptance of diversity; **Action researcher** surveying stakeholders' satisfaction, opinions.
Raising expectations and achievement	Varied pace and approach to learning; SEN children reaching their potential; Skilled and confident teachers; Practical teaching and learning resources available; Better use made of information on how well SEN pupils are progressing; Improved data on progress of SEN children who function below age-related expectations (P-scale level); More flexible, appropriate courses and curriculum matched to SEN pupils' interests and aptitudes; Improved transition for SEN pupils between phases; SEN pupils given a 'voice' and more involved in decisions about their education and learning.	**Learning facilitator** advising on flexible learning pathways, using appropriate teaching and learning approaches; **Implementer** of assessment for learning; **Training receiver and provider** on SEN, LDD and inclusion; **Data analyst** disseminating and using SEN data to inform provision, target-setting, curriculum access and delivery; **Transition preparer** enabling SEN pupils to cope with the next phase of learning, liaising with relevant school staff and other service professionals; **Pupil advocate** empowering SEN pupils, ensuring they have a part in setting their own targets, reviewing their own progress, and have a say in relation to their additional provision.

Table 3.1 *(Continued)*

Key area	Main features	Teacher role
Delivering improvements in partnership	Full-Service Extended schools acting as 'hubs' for community services; Prevention to support child and family before crisis point reached; Multi-disciplinary integrated teams working in and around schools; Improved transparency and accountability to parents/carers; Building parents' confidence in mainstream education for SEN children; Monitoring progress and supporting improvement in school self-evaluation and regular review of effectiveness of SEN provision; Benchmarking and national data to provide comparative data on SEN performance.	**Supporter** of the work of the paraprofessional team in and around school; **Parents'/carers' advocate** mediating, negotiating and listening to parents; **Quality assurer** monitoring and evaluating SEN pupil outcomes (attainment, progress and achievements).

Implications for the role of the teacher

In *Removing Barriers to Achievement* the government confirmed the role of qualified and trainee teachers:

> We want to see all teachers having the skills and confidence – and access to specialist advice where necessary – to help children with SEN to reach their potential.

> Every teacher should expect to teach children with SEN ... ensure the approach to the training and development of teachers on SEN issues takes account of the wider reform strategy for the children's workforce to be developed following *Every Child Matters*.
>
> (DfES 2004m: 3.9)

The government expects Initial Teacher Training (ITT) to provide a good grounding in the core skills needed for teaching in today's diverse classrooms, which includes:

- planning and teaching for inclusion and access to the curriculum;
- behaviour management and awareness of the emotional and mental health needs of pupils (to build their self-esteem as learners);
- assessment for learning (learning skills);
- an understanding of where professional advice may be needed.

> (ibid.: 3.10)

In its HMI report which focused on how mainstream schools were catering effectively for a wider range of pupils' needs in the context of the government's inclusion framework, OFSTED (2004) identified the following issues which schools still need to address:

- increased acceptance and inclusion of pupils in mainstream schools with behavioural, emotional and social difficulties;
- improved attendance and reduced exclusion rates for pupils with SEN;
- increased teacher expectations in relation to the achievements and progress of pupils with SEN;

- improved standards in the teaching of pupils with SEN;
- increased collection, use and analysis of pupil performance data for pupils with SEN to better inform teaching and target-setting;
- increased monitoring and evaluation of the impact of additional interventions and provision on outcomes for pupils with SEN;
- improved deployment of teaching assistants in schools to maximise their effectiveness;
- increased partnership working between special and mainstream schools.

In its review of the Graduate Teacher Programme OFSTED (2005c) found that:

> Differentiation and assessment for learning were relatively weak for both primary and secondary trainees... Trainees were often insecure in planning for the range of ability in the class and did not know how to provide challenge for higher attaining pupils.
>
> (OFSTED 2005c: 53)

OFSTED uses the term 'learning difficulties and/or disabilities' (LDD) to refer to a wider diversity of children and young people in schools, besides those with special educational needs (SEN).

Schools, according to OFSTED, currently identify one in five children as having difficulty in learning of such a kind that he/she needs some form of extra help in class. In their strategy for SEN the DfES (2004m) identifies one in six children as having SEN. Not all of those children identified as having a difficulty in learning can be truly described as having special educational needs (SEN). Once they are given the necessary additional literacy and numeracy intervention programmes, some of these lower attaining and below average pupils reach the national expectations at the end of their key stage. It should, therefore, not be assumed that children who are making slower progress must necessarily have SEN, e.g. pupils learning English as an additional language (EAL).

The aims of the government's strategy for SEN

The purpose and intention of *Removing Barriers to Achievement* is to:

- personalise learning for all children;
- make education more innovative and responsive to the diverse needs of individual children;
- raise the achievement of children with SEN;
- enable children with SEN to achieve their full potential;
- enable SEN children to have regular opportunities to learn, play and develop alongside their peers within their local community of schools;
- give parents the confidence in knowing that their child's needs will be met effectively in school.

The government's strategy for SEN focuses on four key areas:

1 **Early intervention** – to ensure children who have difficulties learning receive the help they need as soon as possible and that parents of children with SEN and disabilities have access to suitable childcare.

2 **Removing barriers to learning** – by embedding inclusive practice in every school and Early Years setting.

3 **Raising expectations and achievement** – by developing teachers' skills and strategies for meeting the needs of children with SEN and sharpening the focus on the progress children make.

4 **Delivering improvements in partnership** – taking a hands-on approach to improvement so that parents can be confident that their child will get the education he/she needs.

Early intervention

Personalised co-ordinated multi-disciplinary services based around the needs of the child; their impact on the learning and well-being of pupils with SEN is a key focus to the first chapter of *Removing Barriers to Achievement* (RBA).

Class and subject teachers will have access to SEN specialists working as part of a paraprofessional team within and across a network of schools, to support and deliver personalised learning. The school's inclusion co-ordinator (INCO) or manager and the special educational needs co-ordinator (SENCO) will co-ordinate and bring such a team together, in order to intervene early and address the individual needs of SEN pupils.

Teachers and Early Years practitioners will be able to spend more time supporting early identification and intervention and less time on SEN paperwork. National strategy training provides teachers with the necessary skills and knowledge to know how to respond to SEN pupils' needs, and at what point to seek specialist advice.

Removing barriers to learning

The government's strategy for SEN is full of good intentions, which link closely with the Change for Children programme, as set out in *Every Child Matters*. As an action programme, RBA has already started to make steady progress in ensuring that children with less significant needs, which includes those with moderate learning difficulties (MLD), who often have their needs overlooked in mainstream schools, and those with less severe behavioural, emotional and social difficulties (BESD), are able to have their needs met in a mainstream environment. The production of inclusion and SEN training materials, as part of the National Primary Strategy and the Key Stage 3 Strategy (now the Secondary Strategy) to support teachers' skill and confidence development, has played a significant part in supporting this initiative.

The government clearly recognises that in order to enable mainstream schools to successfully include a more diverse population of pupils with additional needs, which covers autistic spectrum disorder (ASD), BESD, speech, language and communication needs (SLCN), specific learning difficulties (SPLD) and MLD, teachers will require training materials, guidance, information and access to specialist advice and support. However, irrespective of all these practical strategies, RBA also recognises that:

> Effective inclusion relies on more than specialist skills and resources, it requires positive attitudes towards children who have difficulties in a school, a greater responsiveness to individual needs and critically, a willingness among all staff to play their part . . .
>
> (DfES 2004m: 2, 7)

In its HMI report on SEN and disability OFSTED acknowledged that:

> SENCOs identified the perceptions of staff as a major barrier to effective inclusion.
>
> (OFSTED 2004: para. 29)

For this very reason, teachers and other staff need to engage in training that develops their emotional intelligence within the school. The 'voice' of the SEN child, as well as the parents'/carers' knowledge of their child, can contribute significantly to a whole-school staff INSET designed to help raise staff awareness about pupils with additional needs. Ideally, an approach, which starts from the SEN child's perspective, is extremely powerful and emotive in helping to change staff perceptions and understanding of the pupil's needs. A CD or video could be produced on a typical school day in the life of the particular child or young person, for staff training purposes, which could be viewed as a whole staff or on an individual basis by staff and governors.

The content of such INSET sessions might include:

- SEN pupils introducing themselves – nature of their learning difficulty and/or disability, their age, how many in their family, how long they have had their learning difficulty or disability, how they manage outside school, at home and in the local community;
- explanation of the barriers to learning and participation they face, from their perspective within the classroom, across the curriculum, around the school generally, and on educational visits, residential experiences and in out-of-hours learning activities;
- how, from the pupils' perspective, these barriers could be removed by teachers, TAs and other non-teaching staff working in various areas of the school;
- what the pupil expects generally from all staff and pupils in terms of acceptance, respect, fair treatment, reasonable adjustments, understanding and tolerance of difference and difficulties, in order to be made to feel welcome, wanted and valued as a member of the school and of the wider community, without being singled out or made to feel different to other peers and therefore more vulnerable and susceptible to bullying from others.

Bringing past pupils with learning difficulties and/or disabilities back to the school, who have overcome barriers to learning and participation, provides staff and pupils with positive role models of disability, helping to change attitudes to disability by winning over 'hearts and minds'.

SEN and disability legislation

The SEN and Disability Act 2001 amended the Disability Discrimination Act 1995, creating new duties for schools and teachers:

- not to treat disabled children and young people **less favourably**;
- make **reasonable adjustments** to ensure that disabled children and young people are not placed at a substantial disadvantage compared to able-bodied peers;
- contribute towards improving accessibility arrangements:
  - improving access to the physical environment;
  - increasing curriculum and out-of-hours learning access;
  - improving access to written information using alternative formats.

The Disability and Discrimination Act 2005 stated that:

- schools are to take action to improve educational outcomes for disabled children to address underachievement;
- schools have a duty to promote disability equality in order to eliminate unlawful discrimination, harassment, and promote equal opportunities and positive attitudes towards disability;
- senior and middle managers in schools to take account of disability equality in their policy-making and provision;
- schools to collect and analyse their disability data in order to identify progress made towards improving access to physical, environmental, curriculum/extra-curricular activities and the provision of written materials in alternative formats.

For the purpose of both Acts:

> A child or young person is disabled if they have a physical (including sensory), intellectual or mental impairment which has a substantial and long-term adverse effect on their ability to carry out normal day-to-day activities.

This broad definition covers children with severe dyslexia, diabetes, epilepsy, asthma, AIDS, progressive conditions such as muscular dystrophy, severe disfigurements and incontinence.

The effect of any disability must last at least a year or more. Many children who have SEN are also likely to have a disability; however, some children with a disability may not have SEN, e.g. those with asthma, arthritis or diabetes.

It is heartening to see that the government recognises that there will always be a group of children with more complex and severe special educational needs, e.g. PMLD, SLD, BESD, ASD, who require specialist provision, and who are unable to participate full-time in a mainstream school context. However, that does not preclude them from engaging in some meaningful and relevant mainstream learning and social inclusion experiences, or from their specialist provision being co-located with and on the same site as a mainstream school.

Some special school pupils are dual registered, spending over 51 per cent of their time each week in a mainstream setting. Teachers will need to become familiar with smaller stepped assessment for learning (P-scales, PIVATS, B Squared and Equals) for SEN pupils with more severe learning difficulties. In partnership with key outreach staff from the special school, class teachers will need to feel confident about utilising appropriate teaching strategies and assessment for learning in order to ensure such pupils are able to access the curriculum at the appropriate level.

Such change does not happen overnight, and there must be a realisation on behalf of senior managers in mainstream schools and among professionals in local authority Children's Services that teachers will require the necessary support and time for capacity building in order to develop the essential knowledge and skills to meet a wider diversity of pupils with additional needs in mainstream schools and Early Years settings. In addition, teachers will need to develop their confidence, competence and capability to understand and meet the needs of a diversity of pupils with learning difficulties and/or disabilities effectively in the mainstream classroom by adopting a coaching and mentoring training approach.

In relation to removing barriers to learning RBA states:

> Inclusion is about much more than the type of school that children attend; it is about the quality of their experience; how they are helped to learn, achieve and participate fully in the life of the school.

> (DfES 2004m: 25)

They go on to add:

> Schools and early years settings still vary enormously in their experience in working with children with SEN, and in the specialist expertise and resources available to them from other schools, local authority education and social services, health and voluntary organisations. *Every Child Matters* recognises the need to bring specialist services together, working in multi-disciplinary teams, to focus on the needs of the child.

> (ibid.: 25)

The notion of the paraprofessional multi-disciplinary team has echoes of the medical model, i.e. SEN pupils can only have their needs fully met, 'treated', 'cured' by the 'experts' (paraprofessionals) taking the onus and responsibility away from the class or subject teacher. Paraprofessionals may not just be teachers with SEN expertise, but front-line workers from a range of services, including higher level teaching assistants (HLTAs) and TAs within schools.

Despite this intention to resolve SEN pupils' difficulties via other paraprofessionals, it still does not get to the root cause of children and young people's barriers to achievement, which are outlined in the RBA as being:

> Difficulties in learning often arise from an unsuitable environment – inappropriate grouping of pupils, inflexible teaching styles, or inaccessible curriculum materials.
>
> (ibid.: 2.1)

These barriers are largely the result of school organisational and management issues that necessitate good quality leadership from the head teacher, inclusion co-ordinator and SENCO to address, without making such a situation more complex and complicated by bringing in a team of paraprofessionals to the mainstream classroom. Little consideration appears to have been given to how the SEN pupil will cope emotionally with the range of interventions from different paraprofessionals. The disruption to the lives of children and young people with more severe and complex SEN in mainstream schools is likely to be high. The SENCO is likely to pick up the pieces from this, but it could also be the form teacher or a class teacher. Counselling pupils in such situations may be a likely additional role for some teachers, particularly those responsible for leading on pupil achievement and well-being, whole school.

Raising expectations and achievement

In relation to raising expectations and achievement RBA has already:

- put children with SEN at the heart of personalised learning, helping schools to vary the pace and approach to learning to meet individual children's needs, and develop learning pathways at 14–19;
- delivered practical teaching and learning resources to raise the achievement of children with SEN through the Primary Strategy and strengthen the focus in Key Stage 3 on young people with SEN who are falling behind their peers;
- promoted and extended the use of P-scales to measure the progress made by those pupils working below National Curriculum Level 1;
- ensured that schools get credit for the achievement of SEN pupils (contextual value-added data and point scores);
- worked with the TDA and HE sector to ensure that CPD for qualified, trainee teachers and NQTs provides a good grounding in core SEN knowledge and skills, and that advanced and specialist skills in SEN are part of Advanced Skills and Specialist Teachers' role, along with ongoing training.

Some teachers may become Advanced Skills Teachers, Excellent Teachers or Leading Teachers in SEN or BESD, with specialist skills being made available to other schools, besides their own school. In order to perform such a 'change champion' role, there has to be the guarantee that the teacher will be able to devote two days per week to work within his/her own school and in other schools, and also receive planning, preparation and assessment (PPA) time.

RBA expects those awarded Qualified Teacher Status (QTS) to demonstrate that they can:

- understand their responsibilities under the SEN Code of Practice, and know how to seek advice from specialists on less common types of SEN;

- differentiate their teaching to meet the needs of pupils, including those with SEN;
- identify and support pupils who experience behavioural, emotional and social difficulties.

The Standards for the Induction Support Programme for those awarded QTS require:

- head teachers to ensure that all Newly Qualified Teachers (NQTs) understand the duties and responsibilities schools have under the SEN and Disability Act 2001 and the Disability Discrimination Act 2005 to prevent discrimination against disabled pupils;
- Induction Tutors to arrange for NQTs to spend time with the school's SENCO to focus on specific and general SEN matters;
- NQTs to demonstrate that they plan effectively to meet the needs of pupils in their classes with SEN, with or without statements. (ibid.: 3.11)

The school's SENCO will have an important role to play in supporting, advising and guiding all qualified teachers, including ITT trainees and NQTs, on SEN and disability, and on the implications for classroom practice. Where a cluster or network of schools have employed several NQTs, they may wish to collaborate and provide joint induction inputs and training for SEN, which will reduce the number of separate inputs required by individual SENCOs in each school. However, the SENCO in each school will need to meet with NQTs individually to discuss the individual needs of SEN pupils they teach, curriculum differentiation, IEP target-setting, implementation and link to curriculum planning, as well as giving demonstration lessons to exemplify good inclusive SEN practice in mainstream.

Personalised learning

The government in RBA states:

> We need to provide a personalised education that brings out the best in every child, that builds on their strengths, enables them to develop a love of learning, and helps them to grow into confident and independent citizens, valued for the contribution they make.
>
> (ibid.: 49)

Personalised learning applies to all children and young people and not just those with SEN. It focuses on making education more responsive to individual children by:

- having high expectations of all children;
- building on the knowledge, interests and aptitudes of every child;
- structuring and pacing the learning experience to make it challenging and enjoyable;
- involving children in their own learning through shared objectives and feedback (assessment for learning);
- inspiring pupils' learning through a passion for the subject;
- helping children to become confident co-operative learners;
- enabling children to develop the skills they will need beyond school.

Personalised learning embraces every aspect of school life including teaching and learning strategies, ICT, curriculum choice, organisation and timetabling, assessment arrangements and relationships with the local community. (ibid.: 3.1–3.2)

The purpose of personalised learning is to promote personal development in pupils through self-realisation, self-enhancement and self-development. The child and young person is viewed as an active, responsible and self-motivated learner.

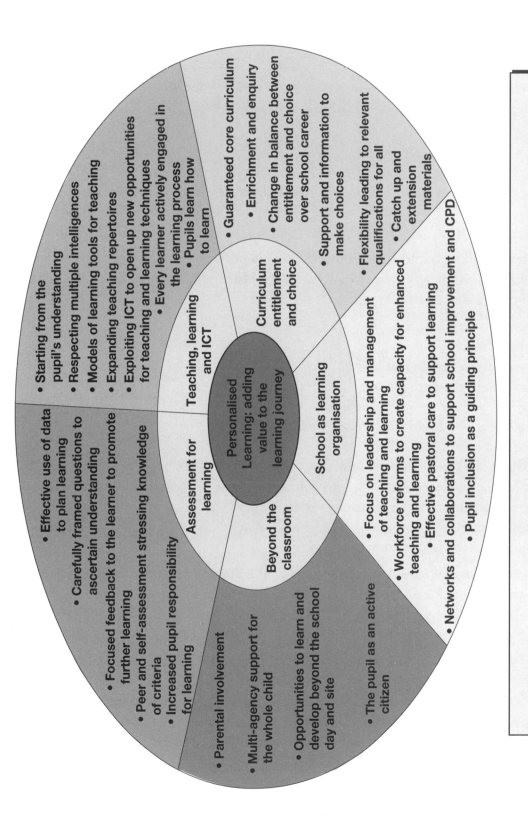

Figure 3.1 Personalised learning. Source: PowerPoint presentation by Graham Last, 'Personalised Learning. Adding value to the learning journey through a whole school approach'. www.standards.dfes.gov.uk/personalisedlearning/Presentations/

Personalised learning will only be successful if pupils are engaged in continual, self-critical assessment of their talents, achievements, performance, learning strategies and targets, so that they can adjust their learning approaches. Pupils having greater ownership and more of a say about what they learn, how they learn, and where they learn best will become a regular feature of personalised learning.

Personalised learning encourages learning to take place in holidays and outside school hours. It is synonymous with inclusion.

The essential components of personalised learning are summarised in Figure 3.1.

Inclusion

OFSTED describes an educationally inclusive school as one in which:

> the teaching and learning, achievements, attitudes and well-being of every young person matter.
>
> (OFSTED 2000: 4)

Inclusive schools are willing to offer new opportunities to pupils who may have experienced previous difficulties. The pupils who are likely to experience barriers to learning and difficulties at some time during their school career are those:

- with special educational needs;
- with physical disabilities (PD);
- who experience gender discrimination;
- from minority ethnic and faith groups;
- who are travellers, asylum seekers and refugees;
- who have English as an additional language (EAL);
- who are gifted and talented (G&T);
- who are in public care (looked after children);
- who are disaffected, have emotional and behavioural problems, or mental health problems;
- from families under stress, or who are young carers;
- who are sick children;
- who are pregnant schoolgirls and teenage mothers.

In *Promoting Inclusion and Tackling Underperformance* (DfES 2005o) the government indicates that inclusion:

- is about valuing diversity and showing respect for all individuals;
- promotes equity and entitlement;
- is a collective whole-school responsibility, which requires effective tracking and monitoring of the progress of all pupils;
- requires individual teachers to think carefully about lesson design to ensure that barriers to learning are removed;
- concerns all groups of pupils who may be underperforming because their personalised learning needs are not being met.

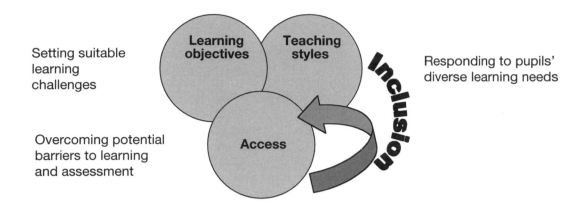

Figure 3.2 National Curriculum inclusion statement of principles for all pupils. Source: DfES (2002a) *The National Literacy and Numeracy Strategies: Including all Children in the Literacy Hour and Daily Mathematics Lesson. Management Guide.* London: Department for Education and Skills.

Delivering improvements in partnership

In the final chapter of RBA, which focuses on delivering improvements in partnership, the government emphasises the importance of schools making inclusion an integral part of self-evaluation. This will be undertaken in terms of monitoring SEN pupil progress/outcomes in relation to:

- the types of setting in which SEN children are taught;
- how fully SEN children are involved in the life of the school, drawing on data on admissions, attendance and exclusions, as well as about curriculum, ethos and attitudes;
- how well SEN children achieve, including value added measures.

As more SEN funding and resources are delegated to schools to support early intervention, accountability becomes increasingly important in order to reassure parents that they can be confident that their child with SEN is receiving the provision they need, with or without a statement, at each threshold on the SEN Code of Practice graduated approach.

RBA clarifies what information a school's SEN policy should include in order to contribute to accountability for SEN:

- how the school identifies and makes provision for children with SEN;
- the facilities the school has, including those which increase access for pupils who are disabled, including access to the curriculum;
- how resources are allocated to and among pupils with SEN;
- how the school enables pupils with SEN to engage in activities of the school together with pupils who do not have SEN;
- how the governing body evaluates the success of the school's work with pupils with SEN;
- their arrangements for dealing with parental complaints about SEN. (DfES 2004m: 4.20)

Every Child Matters clearly sees the promotion of Full-Service Extended Schools acting as 'hubs' for community services, which open beyond school hours and which provide breakfast clubs, after-school clubs and childcare, and have health and social care support services on site, as being a positive development towards inclusion and removing barriers to achievement. Such integrated

Table 3.2 At-a-glance guide to inclusive teaching and learning approaches

AUDITORY	LOGICAL/THEORISTS
CHARACTERISTICS Good listeners, fluent, expressive talkers; good vocabulary; explains things clearly to others; enjoys brainstorming; quick to learn from listening to others. *LEARNS LEAST WHEN:* Unclear guidance on how to do a task is given; or when information is repeated several times. **APPROPRIATE TEACHING APPROACHES** Use audio tape activities; provide opportunities to discuss in groups; give opportunity for oral feedback; use investigative reporting/interviewing; give opportunities for pupils to express ideas in their own words.	**CHARACTERISTICS** Enjoys knowing and applying theories, concepts, models, principles; likes logical explanations; enjoys estimating, problem-solving, doing quizzes and puzzles; works through tasks in an orderly and methodical way. Can identify connecting links. *LEARNS LEAST WHEN:* Feelings or emotions are involved, or tasks are ambiguous and unstructured, or they are 'put on the spot'. **APPROPRIATE TEACHING APPROACHES** Provide step-by-step plans/instructions; use data in a variety of forms; provide a theory or principle to work from; give them time to explore ideas and think things through.
VISUAL	KINAESTHETIC/ACTIVISTS
CHARACTERISTICS Observant; quick to see things others miss; photographic memory; good sense of direction. *LEARNS LEAST WHEN:* Under time constraints, or when they can't see any relevance in the task. **APPROPRIATE TEACHING APPROACHES** Need time to watch and think things through; respond best to visual materials, video and websites; introduce flow charts/diagrams, mind maps, and brainstorming; utilise picture sequencing; visualisation exercises; highlighting text; drawing to demonstrate their understanding of a text.	**CHARACTERISTICS** Enjoys teamwork; doing practical activities; has good co-ordination and manual dexterity; enjoys concrete experiences; learns by example/demonstration/ modelling; remembers by doing. *LEARNS LEAST WHEN:* Passive, or when work is solitary, or asked to attend to theory or detail. **APPROPRIATE TEACHING APPROACHES** Provide opportunities to touch/manipulate objects; build models, participate in activity-based learning; investigation/experimental work.

provision will help to shift the balance of provision towards prevention, ensuring that support is provided earlier before children reach crisis point.

Three key priorities identified by the government in RBA are:

1 to enable specialist therapy staff, e.g. speech and language therapists, occupational therapists and physiotherapists, to support and train teachers and TAs to deliver programmes within the child's school or Early Years setting;

2 to improve access to Child and Adolescent Mental Health Services (CAMHS) and behaviour support services for those children with more complex BESD, including raising staff awareness in schools of children's mental health issues;

3 to improve the range and quality of equipment for disabled children to meet their communication, mobility and daily living needs and support inclusion in school, at home, in social activities or on short-term breaks.

All teachers will need to start preparing now for their future changing role, by acquiring the necessary identified continuing professional development, over the next two years, in order to equip them for this 'brave new world' and 'blue sky' thinking, which is fast becoming reality.

Table 3.3 Teachers' quick guide to removing barriers to learning for pupils with additional educational needs

English as an additional language (EAL)	Gifted and talented (G&T)
■ Use plenty of visual cues and real objects, e.g. video, pictures, maps, ICT. ■ Ensure classroom displays use dual language labelling. ■ Use dual word banks and bilingual dictionaries. ■ Provide collaborative activities that involve talking and role play with peers. ■ Support writing activities by using mind mapping, writing frames. ■ Model key language features and structures by demonstration. ■ Provide opportunities for over-learning, e.g. sentence matching, sequencing. ■ Provide opportunities for EAL pupil to report back to others. ■ Place EAL pupils in supportive groups of peers with good readers and writers who can model English language skills. ■ Provide opportunities for EAL pupils to use their first language, transferring their knowledge to English. ■ Utilise *A Language for All* EAL scale for assessing progress in language skills.	■ Use plenty of open questions and set open-ended tasks. ■ Provide opportunities to use and apply multiple intelligences. ■ Develop pupils' higher order thinking skills, e.g. exploration, reflection, evaluation, prediction, observation. ■ Put extra challenges on learning, e.g. time limit, word limit, devise own crossword. ■ Develop their analytical skills, e.g. investigative reporting. ■ Set a quiz question, puzzle, problem or unusual word for the week activity. ■ Provide opportunities for collaborative group work, role plays, hot seating activities. ■ Give a choice in how they present their work and findings, e.g. diary account, newspaper report, interview, graphical or audio/visual presentations. ■ Seek opportunities for cross-phase and cross-key stage working. ■ Provide emotional support.

Physical disabilities (PD), including sensory impairments
■ Ensure pupils can see the board, TV or PC monitor clearly. ■ Dim bright light in the classroom to reduce glare, using window blinds or re-seating pupil. ■ Ensure safe movement around the classroom for wheelchair users. ■ Ensure learning resources are clearly labelled and fully accessible. ■ Utilise enlarged text where appropriate, or put text on audio tape for pupils. ■ Create a calm classroom atmosphere. ■ Ensure classroom furniture and equipment is the correct height for disabled pupils. ■ Provide a quiet, distraction-free area in the classroom for the pupil to work in, when appropriate. ■ Make use of visual or talking timetables. ■ Produce written information in a range of alternative multimedia formats for pupils. ■ Provide extra time for those who need it to complete set tasks or examinations. ■ Take account that some disabilities (medical conditions) and medication can have side effects that may impair the pupil's concentration, learning capacity and behaviour. ■ Ensure that any pupil misunderstandings, misconceptions and mistakes are dealt with sensitively and positively in the classroom.

Autistic spectrum disorder (ASD)	Behavioural, emotional and social development (BESD)
■ Give one instruction at a time and ask the ASD pupil to repeat this back. ■ Use symbols, pictorial instructions, visual timetables.	■ Catch the pupil being good and emphasise the positives. ■ Give the pupil a classroom responsibility to raise self-esteem.

Table 3.3 *(Continued)*

Autistic spectrum disorder (ASD)	Behavioural, emotional and social development (BESD)
■ Introduce one task at a time and provide clear targets. ■ Give the pupil extra time to process information and complete tasks. ■ Make good use of ICT and musical rhymes/songs to reinforce instructions and learning. ■ Prepare pupils in advance for any change in classroom or school routines. ■ Provide a calm, quiet, distraction-free work area in the classroom. ■ Use simple consistent language, some closed questions and repetition. ■ Encourage turn-taking activities, utilise circle time and social stories. ■ Provide supportive peer partners. ■ Provide a key adult 'listener' for the pupil. ■ Make use of ASD pupil's interests, strengths, talents and skills in teaching activities wherever possible.	■ Refer pupils regularly to classroom code of conduct, whole-class behaviour targets and use consistently. ■ Play calming music to increase work output, where appropriate. ■ Give breaks between tasks by doing brain gym exercises. ■ Provide opportunities for practical hands-on experiential learning, use of ICT and multimedia technology. ■ Use different seating and grouping arrangements for different activities. ■ Allow the pupil 'time out' or a cooling-off period. ■ Create a positive learning environment that adopts a 'no-blame' approach, based on mutual respect and high expectations. ■ Communicate with the pupil in a calm, clear manner, making eye contact and avoiding confrontation. ■ Listen to the pupil, giving him/her a chance to explain the reason for misbehaviour. ■ Use humour sensitively to deflect any confrontation. ■ Keep instructions, routines and rules short, precise and positive. ■ Make use of how, why, what if questions to keep pupils on task. ■ Allow pupils to make responsible behaviour choices for themselves.
Speech, language and communication needs (SLCN)	**Cognition and learning difficulties –** **moderate learning difficulties (MLD)** **specific learning difficulties (SPLD)**
■ Use shorter sentences. ■ Speak clearly and avoid speaking too quickly. ■ Pair the pupil up with a good peer language role model and with a supportive group of friends. ■ Give the pupil simple messages to take to other pupils or staff (verbal and written). ■ Use open questioning. ■ Read aloud and use commentary to improve pupils' listening skills. ■ Use discussion and visual cues to support written communication. ■ Use props to encourage pupils to talk more, e.g. telephone, audio or video recorders, digital camera. ■ Engage the pupil in sequencing and matching activities to develop language. ■ Teach language skills through games, e.g. 20 questions, role play conversations, guessing games using verbal cues, hot seating. ■ Provide a quiet area in the classroom for talking and listening activities. ■ Provide key vocabulary word lists.	■ Allow pupil to work at own pace. ■ Structure learning into smaller steps, breaking down tasks into smaller components. ■ Give step-by-step instructions for tasks. ■ Model what you want the pupil to do. ■ Provide breaks between tasks. ■ Support written tasks with mind maps, writing frames, prompt cards, word lists, visual prompts. ■ Check pupils' understanding by asking them to repeat back what they are to do, or to state three things they have learnt from the lesson. ■ Allow pupils to present their work in a range of different ways, besides written, utilising ICT and multimedia technology. ■ Utilise a range of multi-sensory teaching and learning approaches (VAK). ■ Provide opportunities for pair, group, whole-class and independent learning. ■ Give immediate positive praise and feedback to reward effort and outcomes. ■ Provide opportunities for over-learning to consolidate, e.g. pre-tutoring.

4

New Skills for Teachers: Working in Schools of the Future

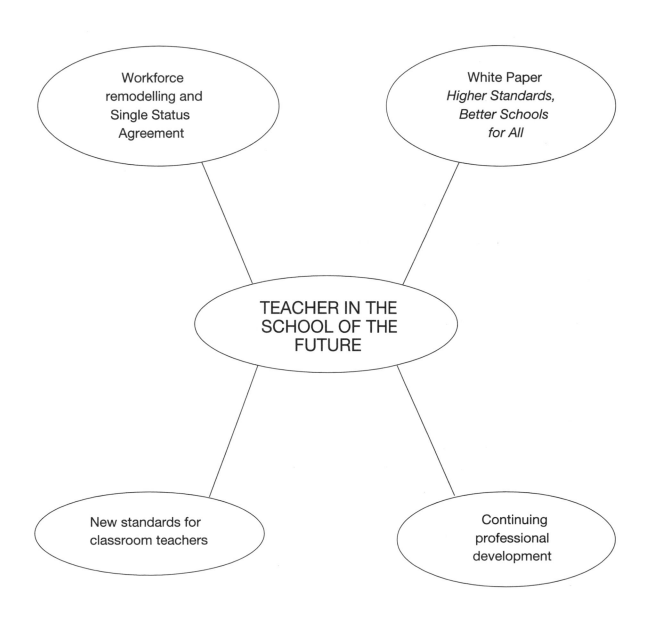

The new professional standards for teachers

The revised standards make it easier to compare the expectations of staff who want to pass induction, Qualified Teacher Status and the threshold. They include standards for Advanced Skills Teachers and the new Excellent Teacher status. The QTS classroom teacher standards underpin all the other standards for NQT induction, threshold (Senior Teachers), Excellent Teachers and Advanced Skills Teachers. All the revised standards place a greater emphasis on equality and Child Protection.

The progression and coherence of the QTS standards have been improved to reflect the changing school context and workforce re-structuring, recognising the distinct contribution that the classroom teacher makes in working with others in a multi-disciplinary team, to progress pupils' learning and well-being in schools and other educational settings, such as Children's Centres. The revised QTS standards reflect the Common Core of Skills and Knowledge for the Children's Workforce, as well as taking into account teachers working with children aged 0 to 3. They also cover legislation relating to safeguarding children in education, SEN and disability, race relations and the *Every Child Matters* five outcomes for children and young people.

In its White Paper *Higher Standards, Better Schools for All* the government commented on its intentions for developing the school workforce to benefit every child. They will:

- train and assess new types of specialist staff to:
  - support personalised learning;
  - enrich the primary curriculum;
  - foster good behaviour and discipline;
  - deliver vocational subjects for 14–19-year-olds;
  - expand out-of-hours opportunities;
- develop new professional standards for teachers, supported by high quality in-school training and mentoring and effective performance management linked to rewards;
- ensure an improving supply of high quality specialist teachers and teaching assistants in Maths and Science;
- expand the Teach First programme to five more cities (this programme recruits top graduates to work in challenging schools);
- ensure clear career pathways and better recognition for support staff;
- recognise our best head teachers as 'National Leaders of Education',
- ensure better support for governors. (DfES 2005j: 8 Summary)

Re-conceptualising the role of the teacher

The implications of workforce remodelling as part of the government's Change for Children programme, bringing in teams of paraprofessionals to support and deliver pupils' learning and personalised services, as well as extending the role of the higher level teaching assistant (HLTA), and the expansion of 'dawn to dusk' extended schools, all place new and extra demands on the classroom teacher.

The professional standards for classroom teachers provide:

- greater clarity about the expectations of teachers at each stage in their career;
- a reference point for teachers reviewing and planning their training and development;
- a structured framework for schools to enable them to make valid, reliable and consistent decisions about the professional development and pay progression of teachers.

The QTS standards for classroom teachers, as for all other teacher status, are set out in three sections, which cover:

1 attributes;
2 professional knowledge and understanding; and
3 professional skills.

The final revised QTS standards will be published in Autumn 2006. These will enable classroom teachers to identify aspects of their role that require further professional development, in light of *Every Child Matters* Change for Children programme. An overview of what teachers must do in order to meet the new standards is provided in Table 4.1.

Table 4.1 An overview of the forthcoming new standards for teachers

What teachers must do to get:

Qualified Teacher Status

- Understand the role of other teachers and support staff
- Take more responsibility for their own training
- Be up to speed with innovations in classroom methods
- Have up-to-date subject knowledge and appreciate how it affects attainment
- Have working knowledge of the curriculum and other initiatives for their subject
- Know national and local assessment requirements
- Be aware of child protection and safeguarding legislation
- Be able to use technology to improve their teaching
- Have a clear framework for controlling behaviour

Performance threshold

- Contribute to and implement new school policies
- Identify opportunities for cross-curricular work and curriculum development
- Make effective provision for talented and special needs pupils
- Guide colleagues on the effective use of assistants
- Evaluate the effectiveness of different management techniques
- Help colleagues to improve their classroom styles

Excellent Teacher status

- Play a significant part in the development of new school policies
- Promote links with parents and carers
- Help set training targets for other teachers
- Have good knowledge of different teaching styles and advise others on them
- Know how to coach and mentor colleagues on work with talented and special needs pupils
- Monitor and evaluate the arrangements to set up to track pupils progress

Table 4.1 *(Continued)*

Advanced Skills Teacher

- Act as a link to other schools, colleges and educational bases
- Be able to apply skills and techniques gleaned from other schools to your own school
- Advise teachers and staff in other schools and educational bases on the most effective way to get the most out of pupils.

Source: Shaw, Michael and Paton, Graeme, 2006. 'More Hurdles to Higher Pay Grades'. *Times Educational Supplement*, January 13, p. 4

Teachers' continuing professional development

All the revised standards provide an excellent reference point for teachers to enable them to review and plan their training, professional development and career pathway. All those who work in schools and other educational settings need to continue to develop their professional expertise throughout their careers.

In their *Teachers' Professional Learning Framework* (TPLF) the General Teaching Council (GTC) commented:

> Investing in professional development is the key to ensuring that schools become whole learning communities where teachers work together, learn from each other and share best practice on effective teaching and learning... It is only through the collective work of teachers, and by creating a shared professional knowledge, that sustained school improvement and raised standards will be secured.
>
> (GTC 2003: 3)

Continuing professional development (CPD) for teachers can take many forms including distance learning, individual self-study, attending externally run courses and in-house training sessions, peer coaching, mentoring and watching Teachers' TV.

Key features of effective continuing professional development

Effective CPD should:

- have a direct relationship with what teachers do in their own school and classroom;
- use external expertise linked to school-based activity;
- involve observation and constructive structured feedback;
- include colleagues supporting one another (peer support, coaching and mentoring);
- provide scope for participants to identify the focus for their ongoing professional development;
- enable staff to be reflective about their contribution to children and young people's learning outcomes and well-being;
- provide opportunities to work collaboratively with other colleagues in the same school or in other schools to share best practice.

The *Teachers' Professional Learning Framework* (TPLF), introduced by the GTC in 2003, outlines the knowledge base and practice teachers require, which aligns with the professional standards for

SWOT ANALYSIS

Every Child Matters aspect(s) to be addressed for professional development:

Strengths	Weaknesses
Opportunities	Threats

Figure 4.1 SWOT analysis for teachers' professional development

teachers. This entails teachers understanding how learning occurs, cognition and intelligence, pedagogy, subject knowledge, teaching approaches and learning styles, and the social and cultural contexts in which these are applied.

The TPLF offers a map of professional development experiences, which helps individual teachers to plan for professional learning:

> Learning runs right through a teaching career. It takes place every day, formally and informally, through a wide range of learning experiences, deepening and revitalising teachers' skills, abilities, values and knowledge.

(ibid.: 2)

Table 4.2 Adapted from GTC Teachers' Professional Learning Framework

Use the following framework to monitor and review your ongoing professional development, by ticking each box as it becomes applicable to you, and place this in your portofolio.

1. **Professional learning entitlement**

   ☐ I have the time to engage in sustained reflection and structured learning

   ☐ I can create learning opportunities from everyday practice, e.g. planning and assessing for learning

   ☐ I have the opportunity to develop my ability to identify my own learning and development needs, and those of others

   ☐ I have the opportunity to develop an individual professional learning plan

   ☐ I can take part in school-based learning, as well as course participation that is recognised for accreditation

   ☐ I have the opportunity to develop self-evaluation, observation and peer review skills

   ☐ I have the opportunity to develop mentoring and coaching skills and offer professional dialogue and feedback

   ☐ I have the opportunity to plan my longer-term career aspirations

2. **Professional learning supporting teachers' practice**

   I have access to guided, planned and structured professional learning that supports me in:

   ☐ Reflecting on and enhancing practice

   ☐ Identifying and addressing areas of pupil underachievement

   ☐ Career development

   ☐ Working with evidence to exercise creativity and judgement

   ☐ Discovering, evaluating and embedding effective new approaches to teaching and learning, planning, assessment and the curriculum

   ☐ Exploiting all opportunities to learn from other teachers

   ☐ Producing, interpreting and managing classroom and pupil data

   ☐ Developing team working

   ☐ Developing behaviour management strategies

   ☐ Promoting inclusion

   ☐ Discovering the further potential of ICT for pupil and teacher learning

   ☐ Recognising improvements in own practice

Table 4.2 *(Continued)*

3. **Supports for professional learning**

   ☐ Working within a learning team, i.e. department, Key Stage, or cross-school

   ☐ Working with a mentor or coach

   ☐ Collaborative teaching, planning and assessment

   ☐ Planning, study and evaluation of lessons and other learning experiences with colleagues

   ☐ Observing colleagues teaching

   ☐ Sharing teaching approaches with teachers from other schools

   ☐ Active participation in self-evaluation processes

   ☐ Engaging in peer review

   ☐ Collecting, interpreting and applying pupil feedback, data and outcomes

   ☐ Observing and analysing children's responses to learning activities

   ☐ Developing resources and projects with colleagues

   ☐ Participating in collaborative enquiry and problem-solving

   ☐ Leading or contributing to staff meetings and INSET

   ☐ Engaging with subject or specialist associations

   ☐ Reading educational, academic and professional journals and texts

   ☐ Participating in courses, online learning opportunities and higher education study

   ☐ Accessing National College for School Leadership programmes

   ☐ Taking secondments and sabbaticals

4. **External opportunities to share and develop professional practice**

   I have access to these networking opportunities:

   ☐ Working across phase or within a cluster/consortium/partnership/network on common research or development work

   ☐ Taking part in local, national or international teaching exchanges

   ☐ Undertaking development with Higher Education partners

   ☐ Networked Learning Communities

   ☐ Contributing to workshops, conferences and seminars

   ☐ Being a member of a subject, specialist or teaching association

   ☐ Participating in local and national steering or working groups

   ☐ Leading or contributing to running professional development courses

   ☐ Developing or moderating examinations or tests with boards

   ☐ Participating in national and local policy development

   ☐ Developing, testing and publishing materials and resources

   ☐ Participating in professional online communities

Source: Adapted from the General Teaching Council for England's *Teachers' Professional Learning Framework* (2003). The full series of leaflets in the framework is available on-line at www.gtce.org.uk/tplf.

5

Teachers as Reflective Practitioners: Outcomes for Pupils

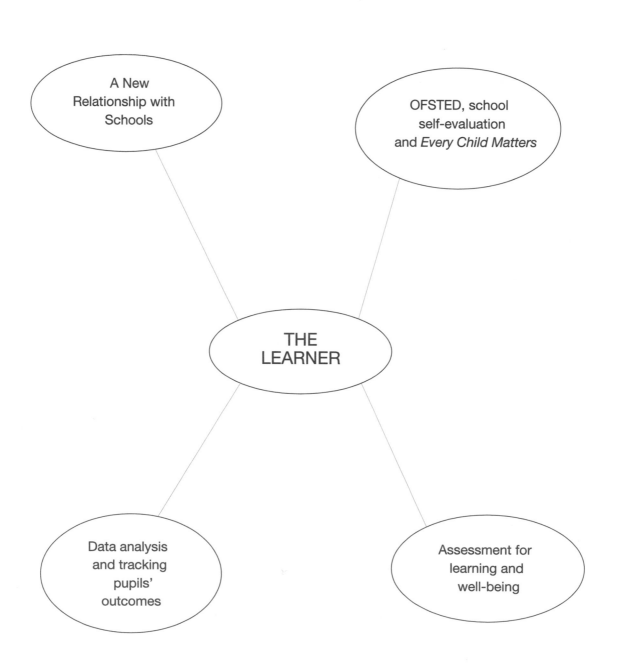

A New Relationship with Schools

The New Relationship with Schools (NRwS) is the relationship between self-evaluation and school improvement. There are three key aspects to an NRwS:

1 an accountability framework with ongoing self-evaluation at its heart, combined with a shorter more focused OFSTED inspection linked closely to the school improvement cycle;
2 simplified school improvement process with every school using robust self-evaluation, informed by an annual single conversation with a School Improvement Partner (SIP), who debates and advises on targets, priorities and support with the head teacher; and
3 improved information and data management between schools, national and local government and parents.

The NRwS process adopts a more simplified approach to school improvement, in an attempt to reduce bureaucracy, while ensuring that every child matters. It was first introduced into mainstream secondary schools in 2005, with mainstream primary and special schools eventually adopting the NRwS model. Teachers contribute to the NRwS process mainly through the school self-evaluation process and data analysis.

Figure 5.1 illustrates the components of the NRwS process.

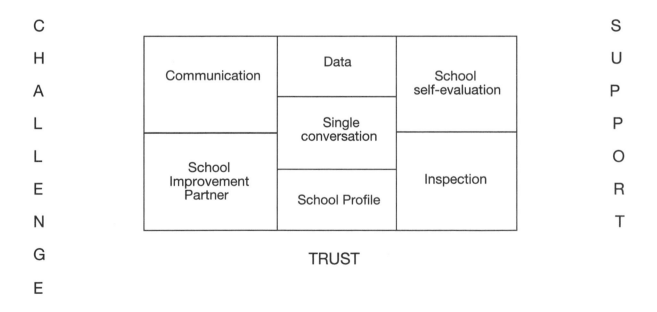

Figure 5.1 Components of the New Relationship with Schools process. Source: DfES/OFSTED (2004l) *A New Relationship with Schools*. London: Department for Education and Skills.

School improvement

School improvement is dependent on good quality self-evaluation. The capacity of a school to improve depends strongly on how well it knows itself. School improvement occurs when teachers recognise and acknowledge the issues they face, i.e. the strengths and weaknesses, and subsequently determine how best to tackle them.

In his Annual Report 2004/2005 the chief HMI commented:

> continuous improvement is something that touches the experiences and enhances the life chances of children and young people on a daily basis.

(OFSTED 2005a: Commentary)

The cycle of school improvement is represented in Figure 5.2.

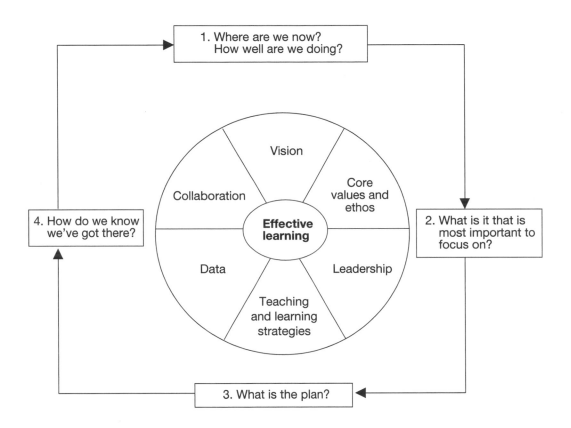

Figure 5.2 The school improvement process model

School Improvement Partner and the single conversation

The School Improvement Partner (SIP) can be a serving head teacher, a recently serving head teacher, consultant/seconded head teacher or a local authority link adviser/attached inspector for the school.

The SIP leads the annual single conversation, which is a focused dialogue with the head teacher, about how well the school is performing and its priorities for the future. The SIP will pose questions, suggest sources of evidence, challenge interpretations of the school's evidence, discuss the accuracy of the head teacher's improvement priorities, and act as a critical reader of the school's self-evaluation form (SEF). The SIP will consider the support a school draws upon from its various partnerships, and what contribution the school makes to the local learning community. In addition, the SIP has a role in enabling schools to share their best practice across the system, within and beyond the school. They also sign off the school improvement grants.

Teachers feed into the SIP single conversation process through their contribution to school self-evaluation.

Table 5.1 New Relationships with Schools single conversation process (Adapted from DfES/OFSTED 2005b: 24)

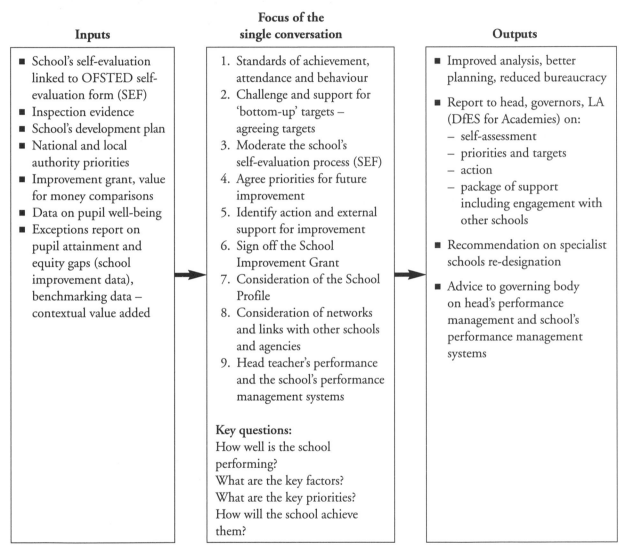

Inputs	Focus of the single conversation	Outputs
■ School's self-evaluation linked to OFSTED self-evaluation form (SEF) ■ Inspection evidence ■ School's development plan ■ National and local authority priorities ■ Improvement grant, value for money comparisons ■ Data on pupil well-being ■ Exceptions report on pupil attainment and equity gaps (school improvement data), benchmarking data – contextual value added	1. Standards of achievement, attendance and behaviour 2. Challenge and support for 'bottom-up' targets – agreeing targets 3. Moderate the school's self-evaluation process (SEF) 4. Agree priorities for future improvement 5. Identify action and external support for improvement 6. Sign off the School Improvement Grant 7. Consideration of the School Profile 8. Consideration of networks and links with other schools and agencies 9. Head teacher's performance and the school's performance management systems **Key questions:** How well is the school performing? What are the key factors? What are the key priorities? How will the school achieve them?	■ Improved analysis, better planning, reduced bureaucracy ■ Report to head, governors, LA (DfES for Academies) on: – self-assessment – priorities and targets – action – package of support including engagement with other schools ■ Recommendation on specialist schools re-designation ■ Advice to governing body on head's performance management and school's performance management systems

The School Profile

The annual School Profile aims to capture the richness of school performance in a way that is jargon-free, user-friendly, easy to access and is powerful in impact. It provides a rounded account of what the school offers its pupils and its community, combining centrally generated data with the school's own narrative. It will provide parents with a broader and deeper understanding of what the school is doing. The School Profile will support more intelligent accountability for the full range of what schools do for every child, including more personalised learning.

The profile will also promote the emphasis in *Every Child Matters* on the need to support all children to develop their full potential. The School Profile encourages an inclusive approach, by showing how the school serves the full range of its pupils, i.e. how it helps pupils achieve their full potential, the ways it supports pupils, and what it is trying to improve. The profile replaces the governors' annual report to parents and the annual parents' meeting (although maintained nursery schools will continue to produce an annual governors' report); it complements performance tables, and increases the flexibility around elements of the school prospectus.

The governing body are responsible for signing off the profile. The School Profile should be in A4 format, relatively short (between two and four pages), and allow for easy comparisons between schools. It is compiled and accessed electronically online and can be viewed on TeacherNet, GovernorsNet and the DfES Parents Centre. School Profiles were introduced in the academic year 2005/2006.

The School Profile contains the following information:

- data on pupils' attainment and progress, set against benchmarks for schools in similar contexts;
- how the school serves all its pupils;
- the most recent assessment by OFSTED, set against the school's self-assessment
- what the school offers, in terms of the broader curriculum, including extra-curricular activities;
- the school's priorities for future improvement;
- what the school offers to the wider community;
- other information, including contextual information about the school, e.g. free school meals (FSM), SEN, exclusion rates, attendance, religious denominations, pupil destinations.

The School Profile gives a school the opportunity to describe:

- its successes and plans for the future;
- the curriculum and activities support beyond the curriculum;
- how the school helps every pupil achieve their full potential;
- how the school is engaging with the wider community, including parents/carers, other schools;
- what has been done in response to the latest inspection.

Communication

Streamlining communication with schools in order to help reduce bureaucracy and support professional development is another feature of the New Relationship with Schools. Web integration (integration of all the DfES's school websites) and online ordering of DfES publications, in response to a fortnightly email, replaces the monthly 'paper batch' of documentation sent to schools. This will enable schools to choose what they want to receive and when they want to receive the information and materials. The launch of Teachers' TV featuring programmes on training and development, classroom resources and education news has supported the ongoing professional development of teachers.

Data for school improvement

The Exceptions Report is used to inform the School Improvement Partner (SIP) and the school, using Fischer Family Trust (FFT) data and contextualised value-added data, which covers social deprivation, mobility, date of birth within year, gender, ethnicity and SEN to identify key variations. Integration of the Pupil Achievement Tracker (PAT) and OFSTED Performance and Assessment Reports (PANDA) into a single electronic system facilitates data analysis and the identification of trends.

County Primary School

17/03/2004

Head: Mr Headteacher, MA, PGCE

Chair of Governors: Mrs Governor

School Profile

Page 1

School web cam

Pictures from around the school

The School's Governing Body

Our Admissions Policy

Assessment

School overall
3
3

Progress pupils make
4
4

Individual development
3
4

Quality of provision
4
4

School leadership
3
4

How we rate our school

How the Ofsted Inspectors rated our school in 2002. To see their full report click *here*.

Our Added Value

National Average = 100

■ Neighbouring schools
□ County

Science
Mathematics
English

98 99 100 101 102

Description: County School is a medium-sized primary for pupils aged 5–11.

What is special about our school? We are a school that supports diversity, in origin and achievement. Our goal is to give every one of our pupils the maximum competence each can achieve in the core curriculum, along with a maturity appropriate to their development to benefit from the wider life of our school and the opportunities presented by their next school. We, the staff and governors, strive in equal measure to contribute to and develop ourselves through our school.

Head teacher   R. Headteacher.   Chair of Governors: B M Governor

Priorities: Our five priorities for the year are (1) complete the re-design of our numeracy programme (2) appoint a new science coordinator (3) have the play area resurfaced (4) develop a 'safe routes to school' programme (5) bring the PTA activities to a new level.

Click *here* for more detail.

Curriculum breadth and depth

In this school children get the chance to learn the basic competences essential to their further schooling and adult life, but in the context of a rounded education appropriate to the twenty-first century. We integrate ICT into all aspects of the curriculum, and in addition give attention to music as a source of harmony in our community.

Extra-Curricular Activities

Our production of Les Miserables   *School trip to Corfe Castle*   *Chess Club*   *more*

Figure 5.3 Example of a School Profile

Our academic achievement

English

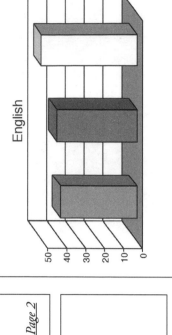

Mathematics

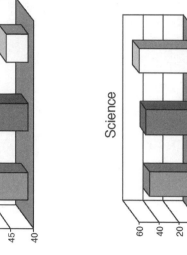

Science

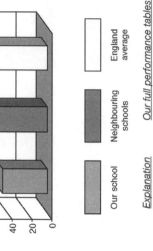

Explanation

- Our school
- Neighbouring schools
- England average

Our full performance tables

County Primary School

17/03/2004

Head: Mr Headteacher, MA, PGCE

Chair of Governors: Mrs Governor

School Profile

Page 2

Community links

The school's links with the wider community include:

- an oral history programme in which the pupils talk to the residents of our neighbouring old people's home;
- participation in netball and football leagues.
- *more*

What Ofsted said about us in 2002.

What the school does well: Progress in English is good in Key Stage 2. The pupils show real enthusiasm for the subject across the school. Over half the teaching was good or very good. The provision for pupils with special educational needs is good. The curriculum is well matched to the needs of the pupils.

Where the school has weaknesses: Attainment and progress in Science and Mathematics are not as good as in English. The relatively small amount of unsatisfactory teaching is mostly the result of teachers not having high enough expectations of what pupils can achieve.

Our school in context

Space for the school to add a brief commentary on the context in which it works.

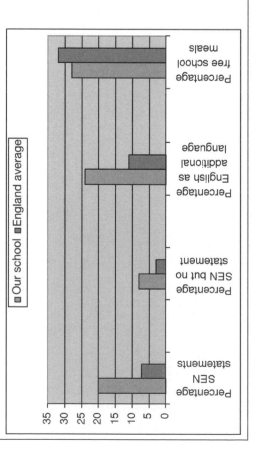

■ Our school ■ England average

- Percentage free school meals
- Percentage English as additional language
- Percentage SEN but no statement
- Percentage SEN statements

Figure 5.3 *(Continued: Source: SHA Conference 2005)*

The key areas focused on in data analysis are:

- the overall standards pupils attain and the standards attained by different groups, i.e. girls, boys, gifted and talented, children in public care, those from different ethnic groups, those with a diversity of SEN and disability;
- the progress made by pupils over time, i.e. how well pupils do between entering nursery and learning in the Foundation Stage, or between KS2 and KS4, or over all key stages;
- the progress pupils make in their personal development and well-being, including the five outcomes of *Every Child Matters*.

Data analysis on attendance, exclusions and pupil destinations will contribute to judgements in relation to *Every Child Matters* outcomes, along with inspection outcomes and school self-evaluation evidence – pupil outcomes especially in relation to health, behaviour, attendance and engagement. When tracking pupil progress teachers need to explore why some groups of pupils do better than others, who may underachieve.

Data analysis questions for teachers

- What is the pupil level data telling you about standards?
- Are there any surprises?
- Are pupils making sufficient rates of progress in relation to their prior attainment, ability and additional needs?
- Are there any trends or issues identified from your data analysis of pupil performance that require further attention? For example, underachieving groups of pupils.
- If there are trends or issues, how do you intend to move forward on addressing these?
- What is the correlation between contextual factors and pupils' attainment, progress and achievements in relation to learning, behaviour and well-being? For example, attendance, exclusions, gender, looked after children, summer-born pupils, additional support or interventions from teaching assistants, Learning Mentors or external agency practitioners.
- Is the educational and personal welfare of the children central to the actions taken?

Individual pupil progress and achievement data are at the heart of school improvement and inclusion. OFSTED commented in *Evaluating Educational Inclusion*:

> the most effective schools do not take educational inclusion for granted. They constantly monitor and evaluate the progress each pupil makes . . . They take practical steps – in the classroom and beyond – to meet pupils' needs effectively and they promote tolerance and understanding in a diverse society.
>
> (OFSTED 2000: 4)

Assessment for learning and well-being

Assessment for learning and well-being, which is a key component of personalised learning, is a process of seeking and interpreting evidence for use by learners and their teachers to decide where the learners are in their learning and well-being, where they need to go and how best to get there.

Data for pupil well-being, behaviour and personal and social development

Teachers need to look more holistically at the achievements of the 'whole child', beyond academic attainment, in the context of recording the *Every Child Matters* outcomes for children and young people. Detailed analysis by teachers of pupils' performance data for learning and well-being leads to the more effective targeting of additional support and the use of appropriate personalised learning approaches.

A range of national complementary assessment systems are available to teachers for recording aspects of pupils' personal, social and emotional development; their behaviour; and well-being. These are outlined briefly in the following sections for teachers to utilise.

Assessment criteria for measuring emotional and behavioural development

In 2001 the QCA issued national criteria for tracking and assessing pupil progress in relation to three aspects of behaviour: learning, conduct and emotional behaviour. The assessment criteria which support the school improvement process can be used with pupils aged 5 to 16, in mainstream, special schools and Pupil Referral Units (PRUs), who are identified as having emotional and behavioural difficulties (EBD). The criteria adopt a positive approach, being pupil-friendly, and support the target-setting process at individual, group and class levels.

The purpose of the assessment criteria is to support schools and teachers in identifying EBD underachievers, improving pupils' behaviour and emotional development, and in removing barriers to learning that may adversely impact on the emotional and behavioural development of pupils, e.g. school culture and organisation, classroom environment, inappropriate teaching styles, or poorly differentiated and inappropriate curriculum.

Each of the three aspects of behaviour has five performance indicator items. Each item (performance indicator) is rated on a six-point scale: 0 = not at all; 1 = rarely; 2 = sometimes; 3 = fairly often; 4 = often; 5 = always. Each of the three behaviour aspects gives a score range between 0 and 25. The three behaviour aspects can produce a maximum total score of 75, and an overall pupil score within the range of 0 to 75.

Assessment using the criteria should be carried out at the end of a term, over a three-month period, in one sitting. Moderation and standardisation between teachers and teaching assistants in the school of the score ratings for pupils is essential, in order to ensure consistency and validity in staff judgements.

Table 5.2 Emotional and behavioural development assessment criteria (Source: QCA 2001b)

Desirable behaviour aspects and items (performance indicators)	Not at all (0)	Rarely (1)	Sometimes (2)	Fairly often (3)	Often (4)	Always (5)
LEARNING BEHAVIOUR 1. **Is attentive and has an interest in schoolwork** e.g. not easily distracted, completes work, keeps on task and concentrates, has good motivation, shows interest, enjoys schoolwork.						
2. **Good learning organisation** e.g. works systematically, at a reasonable pace, knows when to move on to the next activity or stage, can make choices, is organised.						

Table 5.2 (*Continued*)

Desirable behaviour aspects and items (performance indicators)	Not at all (0)	Rarely (1)	Sometimes (2)	Fairly often (3)	Often (4)	Always (5)
3. **Is an effective communicator** e.g. speech is coherent, thinks before answering.						
4. **Works efficiently in a group** e.g. takes part in discussions, contributes readily to group tasks, listens well in groups, works collaboratively.						
5. **Seeks help where necessary** e.g. can work independently until there is a problem that cannot be solved without the teacher's or TA's intervention.						
CONDUCT BEHAVIOUR 6. **Behaves respectfully towards staff** e.g. respects staff and answers them politely, does not interrupt or deliberately annoy, does not show verbal aggression.						
7. **Shows respect to other pupils** e.g. interacts with other pupils politely and thoughtfully, does not tease, call names, swear, use psychological intimidation.						
8. **Only interrupts and seeks attention appropriately** e.g. behaves in ways warranted by the classroom activity, does not disrupt unnecessarily, or distract or interfere with others, does not pass notes, talk when others are talking, does not seek unwarranted attention.						
9. **Is physically peaceable** e.g. is not physically aggressive, avoids fights, is pleasant to other pupils, is not cruel or spiteful, does not strike out in temper.						
10. **Respects property** e.g. values and looks after property, does not damage or destroy property and does not steal.						
EMOTIONAL BEHAVIOUR 11. **Has empathy** e.g. is tolerant of others, shows understanding and sympathy, is considerate.						
12. **Is socially aware** e.g. interacts appropriately with others, is not a loner or isolated, reads social situations well.						
13. **Is happy** e.g. has fun when appropriate, smiles, laughs, is cheerful, is not tearful or depressed.						

Table 5.2 *(Continued)*

Desirable behaviour aspects and items (performance indicators)	Not at all (0)	Rarely (1)	Sometimes (2)	Fairly often (3)	Often (4)	Always (5)
14. **Is confident** e.g. is not anxious, has high self-esteem, is relaxed, does not fear failure, is not shy, is not afraid of new things, is robust.						
15. **Is emotionally stable and shows self-control** e.g. moods remain relatively stable, does not have frequent mood swings, is patient, is not easily flustered, is not touchy.						

Pupils identified with emotional and behavioural difficulties do not necessarily require assessment on all 15 items in the assessment criteria. The aspect and items targeted for improvement will be based on the pupil's individual needs and priorities, but the recommendation for teachers would be to focus on no more than five items at any one time, from any of the three behaviour aspects.

Every Child Matters acknowledges that pupil performance and well-being are synonymous. The National Curriculum Citizenship attainment descriptors are ideal for assessing the *Every Child Matters* outcome 'Making a positive contribution'.

Other national assessment criteria (P-scales), in Personal, Social and Health Education (PSHE) and Citizenship as well as personal and social development, are designed for use by teachers with pupils aged 5 to 16 with more severe, profound, multiple or moderate learning difficulties, who are functioning below National Curriculum Level 1, or at the lower levels of the National Curriculum, i.e. National Curriculum Level 2 at Key Stage 4.

Inclusion has resulted in some of these pupils from special schools becoming dual placement and dual registered pupils, i.e. where they spend 51 per cent or more of their time each week learning in a mainstream educational setting. Teachers working in mainstream and special schools will find the P-scales an appropriate summative assessment tool for recording the *Every Child Matters* well-being outcomes for these pupils, across the curriculum. Teachers can access the P-scales on the QCA inclusion website.

Assessing English as an additional language

QCA first introduced a national extended common scale for assessing English as an additional language (EAL) in 2000. QCA indicate that:

> All pupils learning English as an additional language, whether they are young children, late arrivals encountering English for the first time, or pupils whose home language is not English but who have grown up in England, have to know and be able to use: the sounds of English; its grammatical structures and conventions; the meaning of words and phrases; and the contextual understandings, including non-verbal features.
>
> (QCA 2000: 10)

The extended common scale of early assessment criteria for assessing English as an additional language supports the principle of inclusion in terms of removing barriers to learning and ensuring curriculum access and entitlement for EAL pupils in schools and Early Years settings. The extended scale describes EAL pupils' English development in early smaller steps, e.g. Step 1, Step 2, Level 1 (Threshold) and Level 1 (Secure), through to National Curriculum Level 2, which marks the beginning of the independent use of English by all pupils. EAL pupils will still require some support and monitoring at Level 2.

EAL pupils are likely to have uneven profiles in language use. For example, some may be able to read and write on entry to school in the UK but be unable to communicate orally; others may be able to speak English but require further development with reading and writing.

It is therefore important when teachers monitor the progress of pupils learning English as an additional language that they track their achievements in English across the curriculum, in other subjects. The cognitive ability of some EAL pupils may be hidden by their limited English competence, resulting in underachievement.

The extended scale should be used to make a first assessment of an EAL pupil as soon as appropriate after he/she starts school. From that point of establishing a baseline, the early assessment criteria should be revisited at regular intervals until the pupil meets the relevant expectations at National Curriculum Level 2 in the four aspects of English (listening, speaking, reading and writing).

Value-added progress

'Value added' is a term frequently referred to in relation to progress made by pupils. Value-added progress looks at rates of progress over time in addition to attainment. There is an assumption that prior attainment is correlated with later attainment for pupils. Value-added measures use point scores, which convert P-scales and National Curriculum levels to number equivalents.

OFSTED uses point scores in its Performance and Assessment Reports (PANDA). Performance tables also utilise point scores, which provide a more inclusive measure, ensuring that every child's progress is recognised by a point score equivalent, however small that progress may be. When teachers track pupil progress, it is often useful to record this progress using point scores.

A pupil's value-added score is the difference between his/her predicted and the actual result. One value-added point is equivalent to one-sixth of a level, or one term's progress. The minimum expected point score gain for a pupil is three points per year. This should enable teachers to obtain a benchmark in relation to individual pupil progress over an academic year. It will also enable teachers to identify pockets of underachievement.

Contextual value-added progress

This compares the progress made by each pupil with the average progress made by similar pupils in similar schools, and takes into account a number of factors:

- prior attainment, taking into account teacher assessment, marks awarded and differences between subjects;
- gender;
- month of birth;
- mean National Curriculum attainment level and distribution of the school's intake;
- school context, i.e. percentage of pupils eligible for free school meals.

Table 5.3 Extended scales for EAL pupils (Source: QCA 2000: 12–15)

Step/level	Listening	Speaking	Reading	Writing
Step 1	Pupils listen attentively for short bursts of time. They use non-verbal gestures to respond to greetings and questions about themselves and they follow simple instructions based on the routines of the classroom.	Pupils echo words and expressions drawn from classroom routines and social interactions to communicate meaning. They express some basic needs using single words or phrases in English.	Pupils participate in reading activities. They know that, in English, print is read from left to right and from top to bottom. They recognise their names and familiar words and identify some letters of the alphabet by shape and sound.	Pupils use English letters and letter-like forms to convey meaning. They copy or write their names and familiar words, and write from left to right.
Step 2	Pupils understand simple conversational English. They listen and respond to the gist of general explanations by the teachers where language is supported by non-verbal cues, including illustrations.	Pupils copy talk that has been modelled. In their speech, they show some control of English word order and their pronunciation is generally intelligible.	Pupils begin to associate sounds with letters in English and to predict what the text will be about. They read words and phrases that they have learned in different curriculum areas. With support, they can follow a text read aloud.	Pupils attempt to express meanings in writing, supported by oral work or pictures. Generally their writing is intelligible to themselves and a familiar reader, and shows some knowledge of sound and letter patterns in English spelling. Building on their knowledge of literacy in another language, pupils show knowledge of the functions of sentence division.
Level 1 (Threshold)	With support, pupils understand and respond appropriately to straightforward comments or instructions addressed to them. They listen attentively to a range of speakers, including teacher presentation to the whole class.	Pupils speak about matters of immediate interest in familiar settings. They convey meaning through talk and gesture and can extend what they say with support. Their speech is sometimes grammatically incomplete at word and phrase level.	Pupils can read a range of familiar words and identify initial and final sounds in unfamiliar words. With support, they can establish meaning when reading aloud phrases or simple sentences, and use contextual clues to gain understanding. They respond to events and ideas in poems, stories and non-fiction.	Pupils produce recognisable letters and words in texts, which convey meaning and show some knowledge of English sentence division and word order. Most commonly used letters are correctly shaped, but may be inconsistent in their size and orientation.
Level 1 (Secure)	In familiar contexts, pupils follow what others say about what they are doing and thinking. They listen with understanding to sequences of instructions and usually respond appropriately in conversation.	Pupils speak about matters of interest and begin to develop connected utterances. What they say shows some grammatical complexity in expressing relationships between ideas and sequences of events. Pupils convey meaning, sustaining their contributions and the listeners' interest.	Pupils use their knowledge of letters, sounds and words to establish meaning when reading familiar texts aloud, sometimes with prompting. They comment on events or ideas in poems, stories and non-fiction.	Pupils use phrases and longer statements, which convey ideas to the reader, making some use of full stops and capital letters. Some grammatical patterns are irregular and pupils' grasp of English sounds and how they are written is not secure. Letters are usually clearly shaped and correctly orientated.

Table 5.4 Examples of point score equivalents for P-scales and NC levels and external accreditation

P3 = 1	P4 = 1.5	P5 = 2	P6 = 2.5	P7 = 3	P8 = 5

(These equivalent point scores for P-scales are from Lancashire LEA PIVATS)

W (working towards) = 3

Level 1c = 7	Level 1b = 9	Level 1a = 11
Level 2c = 13	Level 2b = 15	Level 2a = 17
Level 3c = 19	Level 3b = 21	Level 3a = 23
Level 4c = 25	Level 4b = 27	Level 4a = 29
Level 5 = 33		
Level 6 = 39		

GCSE points: A* = 8   A = 7   B = 6   C = 5   D = 4   E = 3   F = 2   G = 1

Short GCSE points: A* = 4   A = 3.5   B = 3   C = 2.5   D = 2   E = 1.5   F = 1   G = 0.5

GNVQ Full Intermediate: Pass = 20   Merit = 24   Distinction = 30

GNVQ Full Foundation: Pass = 6   Merit = 12   Distinction = 16

Source: DfES (2005) *Primary National Strategy. Leading on Inclusion: Understanding and Using Data.* London: Department for Education and Skills.

Pupil Achievement Tracker

The assessment co-ordinator in school will be familiar with using the Pupil Achievement Tracker (PAT) and can support the teacher in interrogating pupil level data. PAT is an analytical information software package that will enable teachers to make judgements about whether pupils make sufficient progress in relation to their prior attainment. Other contextual factors are also included such as ethnicity, gender, transience/mobility, social deprivation, date of birth in relation to Year group, SEN Code of Practice graduated response threshold, category of SEN and additional interventions used. PAT can record statutory key stage data and optional QCA test and teacher assessment data, in addition to P-scale data. Data has to be imported into PAT from the school's management information system. PAT provides value-added line graphs and progress charts.

School self-evaluation

School self-evaluation is a formative, developmental, in-depth, reflective, collaborative process, focused on the quality of all pupils' learning, their personal development, well-being and their achievements. It offers teachers the opportunity to contribute directly to the process, informing their professional development.

> In improving schools, self-evaluation is embedded in the day-to-day work of schools and classrooms, is integral to effective learning and teaching, the driving force of school improvement and the hallmark of enlightened and forward-looking leadership.
>
> (MacBeath 2005: 3)

Self-evaluation feeds into self-review, which is a comprehensive overview of school quality and effectiveness. Good self-evaluation identifies areas where more work is needed, particularly in relation to improving outcomes for children and young people. It has a sharp focus on outlining actions and analysing the impact of actions taken.

Self-evaluation is a continual activity that is at the heart of the school improvement process. School self-evaluation is based on rigorous and honest analysis of evidence, which includes the

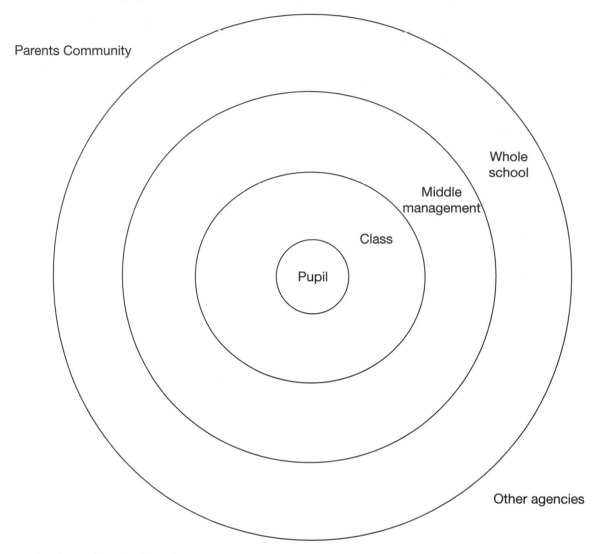

Figure 5.4 Circles of self-evaluation

views of parents and pupils. Rigorous self-evaluation helps schools to improve. It needs to be manageable and integrated readily with routine management systems. Self-evaluation should enable schools to listen to, and do something about, the views of their stakeholders, parents and pupils. It should be an annual process, where the self-evaluation form (SEF) is updated, and includes information about the impact of its action on learners.

The SEF is a summative annual diagnostic recording of the outcomes of ongoing rigorous self-evaluation, fully supported with evidence. It avoids description, indicating key strengths and weaknesses; it identifies what needs to be tackled to effect improvement. All teachers need to contribute to the school's SEF evidence gathering. Teachers need to choose data and information for the SEF that demonstrates the value they add and specify the key actions that contributed most to adding the value.

In order to ensure effective self-evaluation, schools need to provide sufficient evidence in response to each question below.

- Does the self-evaluation identify how well the school serves its full diversity of learners?
- How well does the school compare with the best schools, and the best comparable schools?
- Is the self-evaluation integral to the school's key management systems, i.e. the cycle of development and review?

- Is the school's self-evaluation based on a good range of telling evidence? For example, this should include external evidence, i.e. evaluating the impact of extended services, including daycare, on the learning and well-being of pupils; reports from the school community and external agencies involved in the work of the school and with individual learners.
- Does the self-evaluation and planning involve key people in schools and seek the views of parents, learners, and external advisers and agencies? For example, is the self-evaluation undertaken systematically at all levels: subject leaders, class teachers, teaching assistants, governors.
- Does the self-evaluation lead to action to achieve the school's longer-term goals for development?

Advantages of school self-evaluation

- It is a key driver of success in a school.
- It helps to build capacity for schools and teachers in order to help them respond to and manage change more effectively.
- It goes beyond individual school boundaries, e.g. Full-Service Extended Schools, to provide a collaborative view of quality and effectiveness in relation to an extended curriculum, out-of-hours learning, adult and community learning, and wraparound care services.
- It offers a way of assessing whether the strategies are paying off.

Guidance for teachers undertaking self-evaluation

The National Association of Headteachers (2002) provided the following guidance on undertaking self-evaluation.

- Be clear about what you want to find out, why, how you will go about evidence gathering and what you will do with the information gathered.
- Make the process of self-evaluation clear to other supporting staff, clarifying their role in the process.
- Keep the process as open and transparent as possible to stakeholders.
- Be realistic about the time constraints to manage the self-evaluation process effectively.
- Think small and be specific and focused – don't try to review everything.
- Seek ongoing support and training for self-evaluation.
- Develop a culture where self-evaluation as a process is an accepted non-threatening part of everyday practice.

Inspection

Prominence is given in inspections to evaluating a school's contribution in promoting the five outcomes with which *Every Child Matters* is concerned.

Changes in OFSTED inspections of schools:

- based on school self-evaluation evidence;
- shorter notice of inspection, i.e. two to five days;
- smaller inspection team with HMI involved in and leading the inspection;
- inspection team in the school for two days;
- inspection process will entail discussions with staff, pupils, scrutiny of pupils' written work and achievements; examination of data and assessment records; tracking pupils through a school day will be more prominent than the inspection of subjects;

- inspection covers the four key areas: quality of education provided; educational standards achieved; leadership and management; spiritual, moral, social and cultural development (pupils' well-being), linked to the five outcomes of *Every Child Matters*;
- three-year interval between inspections;
- inspection reports shorter, between four and six pages in length, more readable for parents, reporting on pupils' views, focus on outcomes, quality and impact of leadership and management, clearer recommendations for improvement made;
- judgement criteria on a scale of 1 to 4 (1 = outstanding; 2 = good; 3 = satisfactory; 4 = inadequate);
- two categories of schools causing concern:
  - special measures, where the school is failing to provide an adequate standard of education and has insufficient capacity to improve;
  - notice to improve, where the school is not performing as well as it should in one or more respects but provides an acceptable education.

Guidance for teachers on completing the self-evaluation form

Origins and purpose of the SEF

The SEF replaced the previous OFSTED Forms S1, S2, S3 and S4, and became effective from September 2005. The form is a means of the school recording and summarising the findings of a thorough self-evaluation process.

The SEF asks schools to:

- evaluate their progress against the OFSTED inspection schedule;
- set out the main evidence on which the evaluation is based;
- identify strengths and weaknesses;
- explain the action being taken by the school to remedy any weaknesses and develop the strengths.

The information presented on the school's SEF plays a central role in the inspection process. OFSTED inspectors use the SEF during all stages of the inspection. Inspectors cross-check the accuracy of the judgements made in the SEF by the school with their own findings during the inspection.

SEF coverage

The SEF covers the following areas:

- the overall standards attained by pupils;
- the standards attained by different groups of pupils, e.g. boys and girls, gifted and talented, children in public care, different ethnic groups and those with special educational needs;
- the progress made by different groups of learners over time;
- pupils' personal development and well-being, including how far they meet the five *Every Child Matters* outcomes;
- the quality of overall school provision – teaching, the curriculum, the care, guidance and support for pupils;
- the quality of leadership and management at all levels in the school, including the governing body;
- features and objectives which are special to the school;
- the quality of links between the school and external organisations.

How to complete the SEF (Part A)

(Complete the SEF for your whole-school area/subject area of responsibility.)

- Complete Section 3 (achievement and standards) and Section 4 (personal development and well-being) first, as these outcomes inform the judgements made in other aspects of Part A.
- Use simple, clear, jargon-free language.
- Justify every answer with a brief summary of evidence.
- When responding to the question 'How do you know?', indicate what the evidence is, where it can be found, what action was taken and what the impact of the action was on pupils' outcomes.
- Avoid replication when selecting existing evidence to include on the SEF.
- Provide associated grades for the aspects in the SEF, based on the OFSTED scale and evidence criteria, making reference to the OFSTED document (2005h) *Using the Evaluation Schedule: Guidance for Inspectors of Schools.*

Table 5.5 Self-evaluation form for teachers (Adapted from OFSTED 2005g SEF)

ASPECT	HOW DO YOU KNOW?	EVIDENCE CHECKLIST
1. SCHOOL CHARACTERISTICS 1a. Main characteristics of the learners you teach.	Strengths identified and why.	What is the evidence? Diversity of learners (ability, social background, additional educational needs). Brief summary of learners' attainment on entry.
1b. Distinctive aims, and any special features of the school that you contribute to.	Where can your evidence be found?	Specialist school status; special resourced provision/units; extended provision, additional community services; significant partnerships with others, e.g. for curriculum.
1c. Specific contextual issues or other factors acting as aids or barriers to raising performance in your subject or whole-school area of responsibility.	Action taken?	Recruiting and retaining staff in subject area; recent or impending school re-organisation; mobility/transience of pupils; change in leadership in your subject area.
1d. Any additional characteristics of your school (that relate to your subject or area of responsibility) that you wish to draw to the attention of the inspectors.	Impact of action taken on pupils' outcomes (learning and well-being).	Reputation of the school in the local community for any aspects of its work/provision/extended services.
1e. Outline briefly the main priorities on your development plan, and how they reflect the context in which you work.	Areas for further improvement and action required.	
ASPECT	HOW DO YOU KNOW?	EVIDENCE CHECKLIST
2. VIEWS OF LEARNERS, PARENTS/CARERS AND OTHER STAKEHOLDERS	Strengths identified and why.	What is the evidence? Annual parent and pupil surveys; parent/pupil consultation days and evenings; newsletters, school website for pupils' and parents;

Table 5.5 *(Continued)*

		parents telephone surgery; pupil question box in school; reports on learners to parents on progress, attainment, achievements.
2a. How do you gather the views of learners, parents/carers and other stakeholders about your subject, area of responsibility?	Where can your evidence be found?	
2b. What do the views of learners, parents/carers and other stakeholders tell you about the learners' standards, personal development and well-being, and the quality of your provision in your subject or area of responsibility?	Action taken?	
2c. How do you share with parents/carers and other stakeholders the collated findings about their views?	Impact of action taken on pupils' outcomes (learning and well-being).	
2d. Examples of action you have taken based on the views of learners, parents/carers or other stakeholders, with an evaluation of the effectiveness of what you did.	Areas for further improvement and action required.	Examples of ways in which stakeholders have influenced priorities noted in your development/improvement plan for your subject/area of responsibility; actions you decided not to take with reasons why.
ASPECT	**HOW DO YOU KNOW?**	**EVIDENCE CHECKLIST**
3. ACHIEVEMENT AND STANDARDS (How well do learners achieve)? 3a. What are learners' achievement and standards in their work in your class and/or subject area? 3b. Where relevant: How well do learners achieve in the Foundation Stage? Or: How well do learners achieve in the sixth form? 3c. On the basis of your evaluation, what are your key priorities for development?	Strengths identified and why. Where can your evidence be found? Action taken? Impact of action taken on pupils' outcomes (learning and well-being). Areas for further improvement and action required.	Test and examination results; variations between different types, groups of learners, subject courses, Key Stages; trends over time; comparison with other similar schools; whether learners reach challenging targets; standards of learners' current work in relation to their learning goals; any significant differences between current work and recent results; learners' progress relative to their starting points and capabilities; any underachieving groups of learners; any significant variations between groups of learners.
Overall, how well learners achieve		OFSTED GRADE

Table 5.5 *(Continued)*

ASPECT	HOW DO YOU KNOW?	EVIDENCE CHECKLIST
4. PERSONAL DEVELOPMENT AND WELL-BEING 4a. How well do learners make progress in their personal development in your subject or class?	Strengths identified and why.	Pupils demonstrate considerate behaviour, positive attitudes and regular attendance; how much learners enjoy their education; learners' attitudes, behaviour and attendance; learners' spiritual, moral, social and cultural development.
4b. To what extent do learners adopt healthy lifestyles in your class/subject area where appropriate?	Where can your evidence be found?	Whether learners take adequate physical exercise; whether they eat and drink healthily; whether learners understand how to live a healthy lifestyle.
4c. To what extent do learners feel safe and adopt safe practices in your class, subject area? 4d. How well do learners make a positive contribution to the community?	Action taken?	Whether learners feel safe from bullying and racial incidents; the extent to which learners have confidence to talk to you and other staff when they feel at risk.
4e. How well do learners prepare for their future economic well-being?		Learners' understanding of their rights and responsibilities, and of those of others; how well learners express their views; how well learners take part in communal activities.
	Impact of action taken on pupils' outcomes (learning and well-being).	How well do learners develop skills and personal qualities that will enable them to achieve future economic well-being; learners' understanding of career options, and the acquisition of workplace skills.
4f. Where relevant: How good are learners' personal development and well-being in the Foundation Stage? Or: How good are learners' personal development and well-being in the sixth form? 4g. On the basis of your evaluation what are your key priorities for development?	Areas for further improvement and action required.	
Overall progress of learners in personal development and well-being		OFSTED GRADE

Table 5.5 *(Continued)*

ASPECT	HOW DO YOU KNOW?	EVIDENCE CHECKLIST
5. THE QUALITY OF PROVISION 5a. How good is the quality of teaching and learning in your subject area/class?	Strengths identified and why. Where can your evidence be found?	How well teaching meets individuals' needs and course requirements; the suitability and rigour of assessment in planning learning and monitoring learners' progress; learners guided to assess their work themselves; identification of, and provision for, individual learners' needs; the impact of teaching on learners' progress; effectiveness of management of pupils' behaviour.
5b. How well do the curriculum and other activities you offer meet the needs and interests of learners? 5c. How well are learners guided and supported? 5d. Where relevant: The quality of provision and daycare in the Foundation Stage. Or: The quality of provision in the sixth form. 5e. On the basis of your evaluation, what are your key priorities for development?	Action taken? Impact of action taken on pupils' outcomes (learning and well-being). Areas for further improvement and action required.	Curriculum/activities matched to learners' needs, aspirations, capabilities, building on prior attainment and experience; curriculum meets external requirements and is responsive to local circumstances; enrichment activities and extended services contribute to learners' enjoyment and achievement; learners' degree of self-confidence, skills to achieve economic well-being; literacy, numeracy and ICT provision evident. Care, integrated daycare, advice, guidance and other support provided to learners to safeguard welfare, promote personal development and make good progress in their work; effective deployment of TAs, resources for learning and care; quality and accessibility of information, advice and guidance to learners in relation to courses and programmes, and career progression; effective parent partnership to support learners; contribution of services, school provision to supporting learners' capacity to be healthy (LAC); arrangements to keep learners safe, including child protection, vetting systems, risk assessments, disaster plans.
Overall quality of teaching and learning in your class/subject		OFSTED GRADE
Overall quality of curriculum and other activities in class/subject		OFSTED GRADE
Overall quality of care, guidance and support for learners		OFSTED GRADE

Table 5.5 *(Continued)*

ASPECT	HOW DO YOU KNOW?	EVIDENCE CHECKLIST
6. LEADERSHIP AND MANAGEMENT 6a. What is the overall effectiveness and efficiency of leadership and management in your subject/area of responsibility? 6b. Where relevant: What is the effectiveness of leadership and management in the Foundation Stage? Or: What is the effectiveness and efficiency of leadership and management in the sixth form?	Strengths identified and why. Where can your evidence be found? Action taken? Impact of action taken on pupils' outcomes (learning and well-being).	Leaders and managers at all levels set clear direction, which leads to improvement and promotes high quality integrated care and education; leadership focused on raising standards and promoting personal development and well-being of learners; strengths and weaknesses are known and improvements are made; performance monitoring and improvement to meet challenging targets through quality assurance and self-assessment; how well equality of opportunity is promoted and discrimination tackled so that all learners achieve their potential (inclusion); adequacy and suitability of staff, specialist equipment, learning resource and accommodation; how effectively and efficiently resources are deployed to give value for money; how effective are links with other schools, providers, services to promote integration of care, education and any extended services to enhance learning; the extent to which governors and other supervising boards discharge their responsibilities; leadership and management has the capacity to improve.
6c. On the basis of your evaluation, what are your key priorities for development?	Areas for further improvement and action required.	
Overall effectiveness and efficiency of leadership and management in the subject or area of whole-school responsibility		OFSTED GRADE
ASPECT	**HOW DO YOU KNOW?**	**EVIDENCE CHECKLIST**
7. OVERALL EFFECTIVENESS AND EFFICIENCY 7a. What is the overall effectiveness of the provision, including any extended services, and its main strengths and weaknesses?	Strengths identified and why. Where can your evidence be found?	

Table 5.5 *(Continued)*

	Weaknesses identified.	
7b. What is the effectiveness of any steps taken to promote improvement since the last inspection, and as a result of your self-evaluation?	Action taken and its impact on pupils' outcomes (learning and well-being).	
7c. What is the capacity to make further improvement?		Capacity to improve is strong, evidenced by recent improvement.
7d. What steps need to be taken to improve the provision further?	Areas for further improvement and action required.	
7e. Where relevant: What are the quality and standards in the Foundation Stage?		Children make progress in their knowledge, understanding, skills and personal development; children enjoy their learning and time in the setting; children make a positive contribution to their nursery class and community; children stay safe and healthy, and their well-being is nurtured; children experience quality education and care; curriculum and teaching meet children's needs well; children are actively engaged in their learning; parents/carers' are involved in their child's learning; senior management is effective in promoting good levels of progress, evaluating performance and in identifying and tackling weaknesses.
7f. The effectiveness and efficiency of the sixth form.		Standards, including student retention rates, and the overall progress students make, pass rates, value-added data/measures; independent learning is promoted and effective; standards of students' personal development and well-being, including the capacity for future economic well-being; quality of teaching, and of care and guidance; effectiveness of leadership and management of the sixth form

Table 5.5 *(Continued)*

		in monitoring and improving sixth form provision, providing value for money; effectiveness of links with external organisations and the local community; reputation of the sixth form among learners and other stakeholders; involvement levels of sixth form students in developing the quality of the provision.
Overall effectiveness		OFSTED GRADE
Capacity to make further improvement		OFSTED GRADE
Improvement since the last inspection		OFSTED GRADE
Effectiveness and efficiency of the Foundation Stage, or		OFSTED GRADE
Effectiveness and efficiency of the sixth form		OFSTED GRADE

Table 5.6 OFSTED criteria for school self-evaluation of inclusion (Adapted from OFSTED 2004: 25)

The criteria below contribute to the process of school self-evaluation of the effectiveness of provision for inclusion in mainstream schools. They can provide a useful checklist for teachers

Progress	Curriculum access
■ At least 80% of pupils make the nationally expected gains of two Levels at KS2 and one Level at KS3. ■ 78% of pupils with LDD who begin KS2 at Level 1 in English achieve Level 3 by the end of KS2. ■ At least 34% of pupils with LDD below Level 2 in English in Year 7 make a one-level gain by the end of KS3 and 55% of pupils at Level 2 make this gain. ■ Pupils withdrawn for substantial additional support and targeted interventions make at least adequate and better rates of progress over time. ■ The attendance of pupils with AEN is good (above 92%) and unauthorised absence is low.	■ Sensitive allocation to teaching groups and careful modification of the curriculum, timetables and social arrangements is made for pupils with AEN. ■ The pupils whose reading ages fall below their peers' have access to special help. ■ The curriculum is reviewed annually in the light of a regular audit of pupils' needs and the school responds to the outcomes of the review by establishing additional and/or different programmes of study to meet their needs. ■ Plans to innovate are included in the school disability access plan. ■ Partnership between mainstream and special schools focuses on the development of the curriculum and teaching and enhances the opportunities available for pupils with LDD in both mainstream and special schools.
Teaching and learning	Well-being
■ There is widespread awareness among staff of the particular needs of pupils and understanding of the practical ways of meeting those needs in classrooms. ■ Assessment is regular and thorough and is used to plan future work and help pupils understand how they can improve. ■ Teachers have high expectations of what can be achieved and set challenging targets. ■ Lessons use appropriate methods to ensure pupils learn and enjoy their work. ■ Suitable resources including ICT are available to enable access to the curriculum.	■ There is an active approach to personal and social development, as well as to learning, in the school, especially to lessen the effects of the divergence of social interests between older pupils with AEN and their peers. ■ All pupils learn about disability issues. ■ Pupils have a 'voice' in the school which is heard regularly. ■ Pupils with learning difficulties and disability are able to participate fully in the life of the school. ■ There are well-defined and consistently applied approaches to managing difficult behaviour.

Table 5.6 *(Continued)*

Inclusion policy and practice
■ Admissions and exclusions are monitored and analysed (in relation to placements in other schools). ■ Pupils with AEN whose parents request a place at the school are admitted wherever possible and the school makes reasonable adjustments to include them in the life of the school. ■ There is careful preparation of placements, covering the pupils with AEN, their peers in school, parents and staff, with careful attention to the availability of sufficient suitable teaching and personal support. ■ Trends over time in National Curriculum and other assessments are analysed in the context of available data about comparative performance and are scrutinised. ■ Pupils' work is regularly discussed and the quality of teaching of pupils with AEN is regularly observed. ■ Evaluation of the quality of provision is linked to the information about the outcomes for pupils. ■ Those responsible are held to account for the quality of the provision, and plans to improve the outcomes are implemented. ■ The school integrates its systems and procedures for pupils with AEN (including arrangements for assessment, recording and reporting) into the overall arrangements for all pupils. ■ Deliberate steps are taken to involve parents of pupils with AEN as fully as possible in decision-making, keeping them well informed about their child's progress and giving them as much practical support as possible.

Table 5.7 Teacher lesson observation schedule aligned with *Every Child Matters* outcomes (from OFSTED 2005c, p.3).

Description	Characteristics of the lesson
Outstanding (1)	Almost all learners make considerably better progress than might be expected, as a result of the very good teaching. Learners behave very well and are engrossed in their work. The excellent relationships are most conducive to their personal development. The health and safety of the learners are not endangered. Teaching is based upon an expert knowledge of the curriculum and is stimulating and rigorous. The work is sensitively matched to the needs of individuals and high expectations ensure that all learners are challenged and stretched whatever standard they are working at. Teaching methods are imaginatively selected to deliver the objectives of the lesson, no time is wasted and teaching assistants and resources are well directed to support learning. Assessment of learners' work successfully underpins the teaching and learners have a clear idea of how to improve.
Good (2)	Most learners make good progress and show good attitudes to their work, as a result of the good effective teaching they receive. Behaviour overall is good and any unsatisfactory behaviour is managed effectively. Learners are keen to get on with their work in a secure and friendly environment in which they can thrive. The health and safety of the learners are not endangered. Teaching is well informed, confident, engaging and precise. The teachers' good subject knowledge lends confidence to their teaching styles, which engage learners and encourage them to work well independently. Those with additional learning needs have work that is well matched and tailored to their needs based upon a good diagnosis of them. Work is well matched to the full range of learners' needs, so that most are suitably challenged. The level of challenge stretches without inhibiting. Teaching methods are effectively related to the lesson objectives and the needs of learners. Assessment of learners' work is regular and consistent and makes a good contribution to their progress. Accurate assessment informs learners how to improve. Learners are guided to assess their work themselves. Teaching assistants and resources are well deployed and directed to support learning. Good relationships support parents/carers in helping learners to succeed.

Table 5.7 *(Continued)*

Satisfactory (3)	Most learners make at least satisfactory progress and no major group fails to do so. Behaviour is generally satisfactory and, even where a minority is disruptive, this is not sufficient to cause the progress of most learners to be unsatisfactory. The majority of learners are sufficiently motivated to continue working at an adequate pace throughout the lesson. The tone of the lesson provides a satisfactory basis for the learners' continued personal development. The health and safety of the learners are not endangered. Teaching is accurate, based upon a secure knowledge of the curriculum. The work is geared to the needs of most learners, although some might do better if given extra or different tasks. The methods are soundly matched to the objectives, but are not particularly imaginative or engaging. Adequate use is made of teaching assistants and resources, but there are ways in which their deployment could be more effective. Not too much time is lost. Assessment is reasonably regular, but could be more supportive.
Inadequate (4)	Learners generally, or particular groups of them, do not make adequate (less than satisfactory) progress because the teaching is unsatisfactory. Learners do not enjoy their work and have an unsatisfactory attitude. Behaviour is often inappropriate and not adequately or effectively managed. The tone of the lesson does not promote the development of learners' personal qualities. The health and safety of learners is endangered. Teachers' knowledge of the curriculum and the course requirements are inadequate, and the level of challenge is often wrongly pitched; low demands are placed on the pupils. The methods used do not sufficiently engage and encourage the learners. Not enough independent learning takes place or learners are excessively passive. Assessment is not frequent or accurate enough to monitor learners' progress, so teachers do not have a clear enough understanding of learners' needs. Learners do not know how to improve. There is inadequate use of resources, including assistants and time available. Teaching assistants and parents/carers inadequately helped to support learners.

Evaluating the five *Every Child Matters* outcomes for pupils

Class teachers can begin to track and measure pupils' progress in achieving the five *Every Child Matters* outcomes, aligned to the OFSTED evaluation descriptors.

Figure 5.6 gives an example of five pupils' with additional educational needs (AEN) progress in achieving the *Every Child Matters* outcomes at the end of a year, in a Year 6 class. This offers teachers and paraprofessionals from external services a possible model for demonstrating the value-added progress, over one year, in relation to judging the impact of additional interventions, and informing future targeted additional support for improving pupils' well-being and learning outcomes.

Teachers need to take care when recording the numerical scores for pupils against the five *Every Child Matters* outcomes, as the scoring system used in the model provided is the *reverse* of the OFSTED inspection grading system.

LESSON OBSERVATION EVIDENCE FORM			
Observer:	Date:		Observation time:
Class/Year:	Subject:	Teacher:	TA(s):

Focus

Context

Evaluation

Summary of main points (i.e. strengths and areas for further development)

Judgement on overall lesson quality 1 = Outstanding 2 = Good 3 = Satisfactory 4 = Inadequate

Standards	Progress	Personal development	Teaching	Curriculum	Care, guidance and support	Leadership and management

Particular evaluations related to safety, health, enjoyment, contribution to the community, economic and social well-being to be noted:

Figure 5.5 Lesson observation evidence form

Table 5.8 Evaluating *Every Child Matters* five outcomes for children assessment criteria for teachers

ECM outcomes	Outstanding (1)	Good (2)	Satisfactory (3)	Inadequate (4)
Be healthy	Developing healthy lifestyles is a high priority. Very good provision for and participation in physical activities. Health education valued and believed in by pupils. Very good opportunities exist for healthy eating and drinking. High levels of care alert staff to learners with problems and these are dealt with adeptly. Learners make very good progress in learning to recognise stress. School's support for learners in trouble is very good. Pupils' self-esteem is very good.	Majority of learners undertake two hours of organised PE, sport per week. School has well-organised and well-received health, drugs and sex education programmes. Good facilities exist on site for eating and drinking healthily. Lunches offer a balanced diet and vending machines contain healthy options. Staff are alert to the well-being of learners. Learners make good progress in recognising and dealing with stress and feel they can easily get support from staff when needed.	Great majority of learners undertake at least two hours of PE, sport per week. School has in place a satisfactory programme for health education, including drugs and sex education. Facilities exist for learners to eat and drink healthily on site. Learners are taught to recognise symptoms relating to a lack of mental well-being and have access to support when needed. Staff have adequate support to enable them to recognise health problems and refer them appropriately.	The curriculum and facilities do not adequately promote a healthy lifestyle. Significant number of learners don't have two hours of organised PE, sport per week. Health education provision, including that for drugs and sex, are deficient in range. Adequate facilities do not exist for learners to eat and drink healthily on site, or they are not encouraged sufficiently to do so. Distressed learners do not have their needs adequately supported. Pupils' self-esteem is very low.
Stay safe	Safety of learners is a very high priority. Risk assessments make learning activities safe. Learners feel very safe and know that they are very well supported when threatened by any form of intimidation. Pupils undertake all physical activities in a very orderly and sensible manner.	Good all-round approach to ensuring learners stay safe. Child protection procedures are clear and effective. Risk assessments are thorough and result in effective action. Learners feel safe. Pupils make good use of systems to report bullying, racism, harassment and staff act decisively to protect them. Learners are taught to play sports safely.	Reasonable steps are taken to ensure safety of all learners. Child protection arrangements are in place. Staff undertake adequate risk assessments and act effectively upon them, making sure that dangerous materials and medicines are secure. Learners feel safe, and know and make use of reporting system for bullying. Pupils are taught to swim.	Provider does not take adequate steps to ensure that learners are safe. Learners don't feel safe. Lack of adequate child protection arrangements. Learners are exposed to unacceptable risks, resulting from inadequate risk assessment. Reporting systems for bullying are ineffective. Learners report they don't feel safe.

Table 5.8 *(Continued)*

ECM outcomes	Outstanding (1)	Good (2)	Satisfactory (3)	Inadequate (4)
Enjoy and achieve	Standards are rising very fast or being maintained at very high levels. Virtually all learners make very good progress and enjoy learning very much. Personal development is very good, as shown in their high self-esteem, high aspirations and increasing independence. High quality provision and teaching exist.	Standards are rising fast and compare well with similar schools. Learners make good progress and no significant groups lag behind. Pupils enjoy their education a great deal and have positive attitudes and good behaviour. Learners make good progress in their personal qualities. Provision and teaching are of good quality. Strengths and weaknesses are known and also what must be done to improve.	Standards are rising steadily and are broadly in line with those in similar schools. Most learners make at least satisfactory progress in the majority of subjects, courses and areas of learning. No group of learners underachieves significantly. Pupils generally enjoy their learning as shown by their satisfactory attitudes, behaviour and attendance. The personal development of most learners is satisfactory. The teaching, curriculum, recreational activities and monitoring of progress are satisfactory overall. Groups in difficulty are identified and there are adequate strategies to assist them.	Significant numbers of learners do not enjoy their education and or do not achieve adequately. The quality of provision or the effectiveness of management are inadequate to make the outcomes satisfactory. Significant number of pupils display disaffection. There are marked deficiencies in one or more aspects of learners' personal development. Provision and teaching are unsatisfactory. There is a lack of accurate self-evaluation and ineffective action arising from this.
Make a positive contribution to community	Learners make a very strong contribution to the community. Pupils are taught about their rights and encouraged and empowered to express their views very effectively. There is a self-disciplined community in which bullying and discrimination are very rare, and when they occur are dealt with most effectively. Learners' views are central to the decisions made by the school. Learners have a very high level of involvement in community activities. Citizenship is a very strong part of the taught curriculum and in the life of the pupils.	Learners make a good contribution to the community. They have a clear understanding of their rights, a confidence to express their views and form constructive relationships with adults. Bullying and discrimination are rare and are dealt with effectively. Pupils' views are listened to and they are actively involved in activities that affect the community. Citizenship is well embedded in the curriculum.	Learners have a satisfactory understanding of their rights and a reasonable understanding of how to bring about change. The incidence of bullying and discrimination is not high. Learners express their points of view, and several activities are initiated and managed by them. Adequate steps are taken to listen to the views of pupils, help them to form positive relationships with adults and take on responsibility. Clear policies exist to combat bullying and harrassment, action is taken to reduce incidents of them and victims have good access to support.	Learners don't make an adequate contribution to their community and are not sufficiently encouraged to do so. Pupils have an inadequate understanding of their rights and participation in decisions that affect them. There is extensive bullying and discrimination. There is a low level of pupil involvement in communal activities. Significant shortfalls exist in the citizenship curriculum. There are inadequate mechanisms and action to deal with bullying and harassment.

Table 5.8 *(Continued)*

ECM outcomes	Outstanding (1)	Good (2)	Satisfactory (3)	Inadequate (4)
Achieve economic and social well-being	High priority is given to developing the self-confidence skills of pupils. Challenging teaching styles and a wide range of engaging and demanding activities enable learners to make very good progress in their capacity to handle change and take initiative. Pupils make confident strides in their financial literacy. The area is most carefully monitored and imaginatively developed.	Learners make good progress in acquiring the skills and qualities that will enable them to do well at work. The teaching styles and available activities effectively promote enterprising qualities in learners. Financial literacy is a strong part of the curriculum and pupils progress well. The provision for this area of the curriculum is carefully monitored and continuously improved.	Learners acquire, as appropriate for their age, the skills and personal qualities that will enable them to succeed at work. A range of teaching styles and enrichment opportunities satisfactorily promote these skills and qualities. Pupils make satisfactory progress in their financial literacy. The quality of work related learning is reviewed accurately and adequate action is taken to remedy any weaknesses.	Learners don't make adequate progress in the skills and personal qualities that will enable them to succeed at work. There is slow progress made in acquiring work related skills. Teaching styles are overly didactic and don't enable pupils to develop their personal qualities and skills or their enterprise capability. Major gaps exist in KS4 provision.

Teachers' **Every Child Matters** *model assessment rating scale*

> ### *Every Child Matters* outcomes rating scale (0–5)
>
> 0 = not met at all
>
> 1 = inadequate/poor
>
> 2 = developing in some aspects
>
> 3 = satisfactory overall in outcomes
>
> 4 = good
>
> 5 = outstanding and fully met

The OFSTED assessment criteria descriptors for each of the five *Every Child Matters* outcomes provides a consistent assessment system for evaluating progress at a whole-school, year group, or class level for those pupils who are vulnerable, as well as for those children and young people with additional educational needs which create barriers to their learning and well-being.

Teachers and external professionals would need to collaborate in moderating their judgements about the achievements of pupils against the *Every Child Matters* outcomes, using the descriptors and suggested scoring system. Some of the evidence gathered to demonstrate outcomes for children is likely to be subjective, and teachers and paraprofessionals will need to ensure that they cross-check their evidence with the views of parents/carers, and pupils, where appropriate.

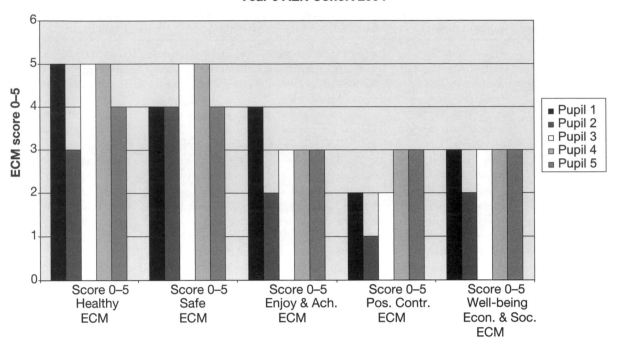

Year 6 AEN Cohort 2004

Legend:
- Pupil 1
- Pupil 2
- Pupil 3
- Pupil 4
- Pupil 5

Figure 5.6 Example of five pupils' progress in achieving *Every Child Matters* outcomes at year end

An *Every Child Matters* model pupil survey for teachers

Every Child Matters pupil survey

Before you start to answer the questions be aware that:

- There are five *Every Child Matters* outcomes for pupil well-being:
  - being healthy;
  - staying safe;
  - enjoying and achieving;
  - making a positive contribution;
  - achieving economic well-being.
- Please answer the questions in the best way that suits you, e.g. in writing, on the computer or orally.

Questions
1. How does the school and the staff look after my safety?
2. What does the school do to help me be healthy and have a healthy lifestyle?
3. What does the school do to make sure I enjoy my learning and achieve?
4. How does the school make sure I can express my views?
5. How does the school and its staff act on my views and opinions?
6. How does the school ensure that I can participate in community and out-of-hours learning activities?
7. How does the school help to prepare me for the next stage of schooling, further study or for work?
8. How good, overall, are the five *Every Child Matters* outcomes for pupils in this school?
9. What else could the school do to make things better for me and other pupils?

6

Managing Change: Teachers Working with Paraprofessionals, External Agencies and Parents

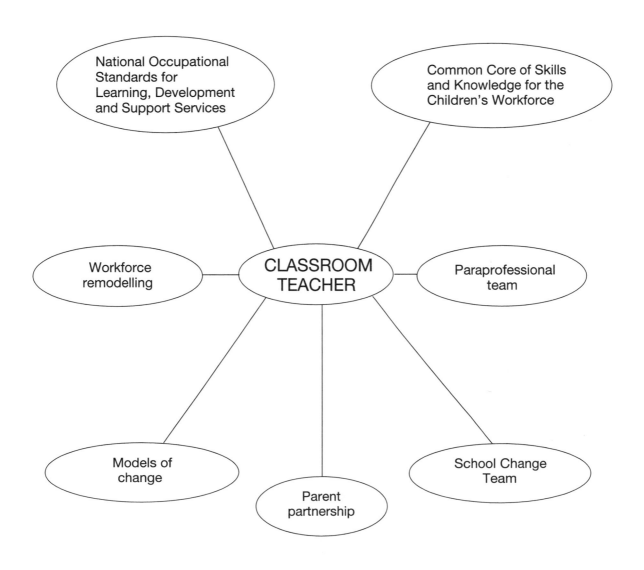

The process of change

The requirement to transform and change schools and the educational system in the twenty-first century has been brought about by the need to develop a different approach to teaching and learning based on learning how to learn, in order to meet the expectations and new demands placed on young people in today's society.

Change is best described as a developmental process rather than as a single event. It aims to improve practice, introduce new policies and functions, in addition to altering the 'status quo'. Change can be a challenging process for practitioners working together from different services (health, education and social services) in and around school sites and Children's Centres. It often entails working in a new way, and moving outside the 'comfort zone', away from familiar practices. The change process has to engage the hearts and minds of all staff in a school. Practitioners therefore need to reassess old assumptions, beliefs, values and theories.

Change and the individual teacher

An individual passes through particular stages in a change process. The Sigmoid Change Curve (Figure 6.1, Table 6.1) best represents individual change. It does not matter whether change is positive or negative, chosen or imposed; the basic shape of the change curve remains the same.

Enthusiasm and a shared commitment promote change, with shared expertise being a key driver of change. To assist teachers and other service practitioners in managing change, each needs to use and understand a common language, as well as understand each other's respective roles. They also need to understand the relationship between the current situation and the future desired state. Teachers and schools need to consider their expectations for the future in the context of the *Every Child Matters* Change for Children programme, e.g. by reflecting on the questions 'Where do we want to be?' and 'How do we get there?'

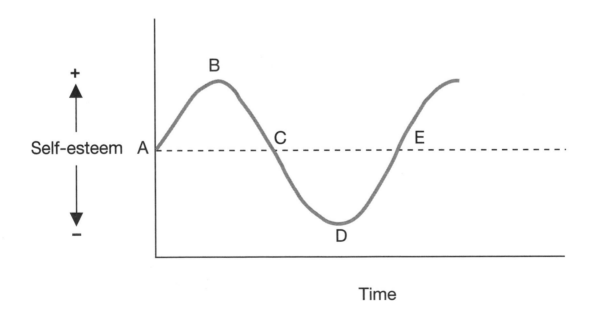

Figure 6.1 The Sigmoid Change Curve. Source: NCSL (2002/2003) *Leading and Managing Staff. NPQH Development Module 3, D1 Strategic Direction and Development of the School, Change and the individual Figure 4: The Change Curve 16.* Nottingham: National College of School Leadership, pp. 24–5.

Table 6.1 Stages in the Sigmoid Change Curve

Stage of change	Strategies to manage change
A. Point at which the change is first announced. Reactions vary between excitement and anger.	Keep well informed about planned change and the effect it might have on individuals. Be clear about the reasons for change.
B. Change occurs with immediate feelings of elation or depression according to how unexpected the change is. Positive and negative feelings.	Support to help individual through conflicting and confusing mood swings.
C. Denial of the magnitude of change with self-doubt and depression sometimes.	Seek an active emphatic listener who will listen to any concerns or negative feelings.
D. Acceptance that the change is not going to go away and that it is here to stay.	Begin to think about strategies and suggestions for ways forward.
E. Practical stage where individual tries and tests out different ways of adapting to the change.	Suggestions and advice are welcomed by others. There is support in looking at different options and testing out the likely consequences of each.

Source: from NCSL (2002/2003).

Local change programmes require transparency, openness and clear communication routes with stakeholders involved in the change process. Successful change is dependent on a clear focus on improved outcomes for children and young people.

Models of change

There are many models available to support individuals and schools through a planned process of change. The models selected are those that best suit the needs of teachers and other paraprofessionals supporting pupils with additional needs in schools and Children's Centres.

Michael Fullan's model of change

This model is based on five key dimensions of change that individuals and schools will go through.

1 **Moral purpose** – underpinned by values and vision with the understanding that the change will make a positive difference to the lives of staff, pupils, parents, governors and the community.
2 **Understanding change** – developing the capacity to problem solve; encouraging others to buy into the change; building the capacity for change through collaborative team building; listening to concerns of those who may have some reservations about the change.
3 **Relationship building** – developing emotional intelligence.
4 **Knowledge creation and sharing** – defining the learning community; raising awareness, developing skills, creating and sharing new knowledge.
5 **Coherence making** – some creativity encouraged to prevent stagnation, but not too much, which could lead to initiative fatigue and overload.

Kurt Lewin's Force Field Analysis model

Stages in the process entail:

1 Define the change needed.
2 List all the possible factors which might support the change – (the drivers).
3 List all the factors which might prevent implementation of the change – (the restraints).
4 Begin to plan for sustainable implementation of change by identifying the strategies and approaches that will help to achieve successful change.

The change required:	
Drivers of change	Restraints on change
Strategies for sustainable change implementation	

Figure 6.2 Lewin's Force Field Analysis model. Reproduced with permission from NCSL. Source: NCSL (2002/2003) NPQH Development Module 3, D1 'Strategic direction and development of the school'.

The change process stages of transformation that teachers will need to work through, in removing barriers to achievement and in meeting the *Every Child Matters* Change for Children programme, entails:

1 **creating the right climate** for risk-taking and experimentation, and removing any 'blame culture' if an idea does not work;
2 **disciplined innovation** avoiding innovation overload by focusing on one or two priorities that can be well managed within a school and across a Networked Learning Community, working in partnership, i.e. high impact for small energy input (SMART working);
3 **going lateral** by spreading new practice on a peer-to-peer basis (coaching and mentoring) through networks, where an initiative or idea is adopted because it will be of real benefit to pupils and make working more effective and better for stakeholders, enabling best practice to be demonstrated in new contexts;
4 **utilising ICT** to complement face-to-face teacher partnership working through electronic communication systems and multimedia technology to support 'virtual' CPD training opportunities.

Table 6.2 Simplified change process for teachers (from Bond and Waterhouse: 2005).

Understand and appreciate	Discover	Deepen	Develop and experience	Deliver
Starting to address issues	This is bigger than first thought	It is tough but a solution can be found	There is a strategy and a plan for future success	Some issues have been resolved and a way forward has been found
Mutual respect	**Commitment**	**Clarity**	**Openness**	**Trust**

Kotter's model of change

This model has been used within the Change for Children programme at organisational and service levels. It has eight critical steps:

1 **Establish a sense of urgency** – identify and discuss potential crises and major opportunities.
2 **Form a powerful, guiding coalition** – assemble a group who will work together as a team to lead the change effort.
3 **Create a vision** – to direct the change effort with strategies for achieving the vision.
4 **Communicate the vision and strategies** – by a range of methods; teach new behaviours through guiding.
5 **Empower others to act on the vision** – get rid of any obstacles to change; change systems or structures that undermine the vision; encourage risk-taking, creativity and innovation.
6 **Plan and create short-term wins** – visible performance improvements that are recognised and rewarded.
7 **Consolidate improvements and produce still more change** – by recruiting, promoting and developing credible employees acting as change agents, who can implement the vision and introduce new project themes.
8 **Institutionalise new approaches** – disseminate and articulate the successful change; ensure leadership development and succession.

School Change Teams

As part of the Workforce Remodelling and Transforming Learning Communities some teachers may find themselves being invited to join the cross-functional School Change Team (SCT), comprising representatives of the teaching, support staff and the governing body.

The purpose of the School Change Team is to:

- share workload issues and views;
- prioritise change initiatives within the school;
- make positive contributions to problem-solving in order to identify workforce solutions;
- act as a communication channel to the whole-school workforce;
- oversee and implement change initiatives.

The Change Team enables the school to become a 'solution assembler' meeting the personalised learning needs of the 'whole' child and young person within the wider local community context. As part of the Workforce Remodelling agenda, the School Change Team can also help to share learning and ideas about staffing structures with other schools and partner organisations.

School workforce remodelling

In 2003, the government signed the National Agreement in consultation with employers and teaching unions. This set out timescales for changes in working conditions for teaching and non-teaching staff. The school remodelling support programme emerged from the National Agreement, which is designed to:

- help schools develop the most appropriate staffing structures to reduce the workload of teachers by remodelling and refocusing roles in schools, in order that teachers can focus on teaching rather than administrative roles;
- support schools in delivering the core universal offer for extended schools in order that all children and families can have access to additional activities and services via their school.

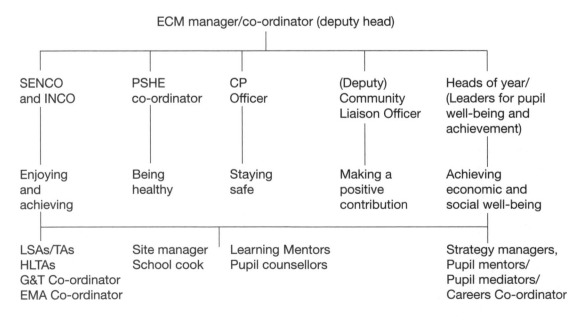

Figure 6.3 Inclusion team approach

The Teacher Training Agency (TTA), now the Training and Development Agency (TDA) for Schools, in its Corporate Plan for 2005–2008 identified that:

> Schools are changing and the pace of change is fast. More people are working in our schools than ever before, including almost half a million support staff. As schools become more complex organisations and offer a wide range of services, the work of support staff is becoming more varied and demanding. There is an increasing emphasis on building the whole school team so that everyone working in a school can contribute to the overall purpose of raising standards and promoting well-being.
>
> (TTA 2005: Foreword)

Practitioners teaming up in new ways, sharing information and working more closely together across education, health and social services, to protect children and young people from harm, and help them achieve, is a key feature of the government's Change for Children programme.

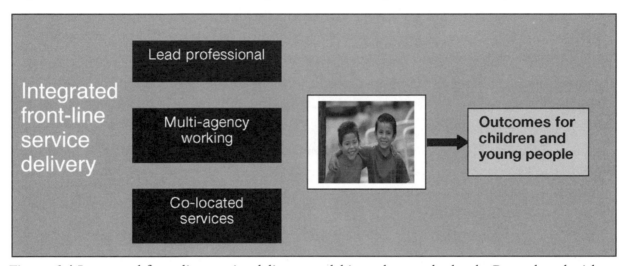

Figure 6.4 Integrated front-line service delivery model in and around schools. Reproduced with permission from NCSL. (Source: DfES 2005q, Supporting the New Agenda for Children's Services and Schools: The Role of Learning Mentors and Co-ordinators, page 5).

Team Around the Child is a model of provision, as illustrated in Figure 6.4, where different practitioners from a range of services come together specifically to address the needs of an individual child.

In its White Paper *Higher Standards, Better Schools for All*, the government identified the wider roles and right mix required of high quality staff working in a range of educational settings:

- a group of leading teachers in every school to co-ordinate catch up and stretch activities (for gifted and talented pupils), within and beyond the normal school day, providing one-to-one and small-group tuition;
- more support staff trained to a high level in literacy and numeracy; and more staff trained in vocational areas, like catering, to come into schools and colleges to deliver the 14–19 diplomas;
- health and welfare staff ready for the new roles they will play in Full-Service and other extended schools;
- trained sports coaches, music tutors and modern foreign language assistants to enrich the primary curriculum;
- professionals with the credibility, recent practical experience and workplace knowledge to provide high quality vocational education. Some of these will be school employees; some will be brought in from employers, work-based learning providers or colleges;

- trained specialists able to deal with disruptive behaviour, truancy and pastoral issues;
- trained bursars and other administrative staff, freeing teachers to teach and ensuring the best use of resources to improve outcomes for children. (DfES 2005j: 8.15)

There will be a greater sharing of staff across schools and between schools, colleges and business as part of the modernisation of the school system. The new National Standards for classroom teachers highlight the distinctive contribution of the teacher in the context of wider multi-disciplinary team working. They also reflect the Common Core of Skills and Knowledge for the Children's Workforce. Teachers need to be clear about the roles of different paraprofessionals working in the classroom and schools, to support pupils' personalised learning and well-being.

Working with other professionals and practitioners

Paraprofessionals

A paraprofessional is an individual with knowledge and training who performs important service delivery activities to support pupils' personalised learning and well-being, working as part of a multi-disciplinary team, within one school or across a range of educational settings.

The paraprofessional team can comprise specialist teachers, school support staff (TAs, HLTAs, Learning Mentors), as well as health care and social services staff who provide therapeutic inputs, interventions and support for children and young people, in order to remove barriers to learning.

Class teachers need to be able to demonstrate the effective deployment of additional supporting adults in the classroom, and have evidence of the impact of this additional support on pupil outcomes, i.e. the *Every Child Matters* five outcomes for children and young people.

The National Occupational Standards for Learning, Development and Support Services

The 61 National Occupational Standards and qualifications framework for Learning, Development and Support Services (2004) describe the minimum standards of competences, knowledge, understanding and actions for effective working by Education Welfare Officers, Learning Mentors and Connexions Personal Advisers. The welfare of children and young people they work with is paramount to their role. Practitioners adopt a client-centred approach based on equality, inclusion, access, honesty, trust and respect. Practitioners are committed to working in partnership with other individuals and agencies to improve the life chances of children and young people.

The Common Core of Skills and Knowledge for the Children's Workforce

The Common Core of Skills and Knowledge for the Children's Workforce reflects a set of common values for practitioners that promote equality and inclusion, respect diversity and challenge stereotypes, helping to improve the life chances of children and young people.

The common core for the Children's Workforce sets out the basic skills and knowledge required by practitioners (including volunteers) whose work brings them into regular contact with children, young people and their families. They cover the aspects of work of service staff, working directly or indirectly with children, young people and their families. These include police officers, doctors, dentists, nurses, teachers, nursery staff, social workers, therapists, youth workers, leisure and recreational workers, housing staff, and those staff who work in criminal/youth justice, mental health or drug and alcohol services.

The Common Core of Skills and Knowledge are designed to enable multi-disciplinary teams to work together more effectively in the interests of the child and young person.

There are six areas of expertise in the Common Core of Skills and Knowledge for the Children's Workforce:

1. Effective communication and engagement with children, young people and families.
2. Child and young person development.
3. Safeguarding and promoting the welfare of the child.
4. Supporting transitions.
5. Multi-agency working.
6. Sharing information.

Table 6.3 Common Core of Skills and Knowledge for the Children's Workforce

1. Effective communication and engagement with children, young people, their families and carers	4. Supporting transitions
Skills: ■ Listening and building empathy ■ Summarising and explaining ■ Consultation and negotiation Knowledge: ■ How communication works ■ Confidentiality and ethics ■ Sources of support ■ Importance of respect	Skills: ■ Identify transitions ■ Provide support Knowledge: ■ How children and young people respond to change ■ When and how to intervene
2. Child and young person development	5. Multi-agency working
Skills: ■ Observation and judgement ■ Empathy and understanding Knowledge: ■ Understand context ■ Understand how babies, children and young people develop ■ Be clear about own job role, i.e. who to call upon for expertise and report concerns to ■ Know how to reflect and improve	Skills: ■ Communication and teamwork – with other professionals, practitioners ■ Assertiveness, i.e. be proactive, challenge, be objective, know when to refer to others Knowledge: ■ Role and remit of self and of other team colleagues ■ Know how to make queries ■ Procedures and working methods, i.e. know CAF, and how other services operate ■ The law, policies and procedures
3. Safeguarding and promoting the welfare of the child	6. Sharing information
Skills: ■ Relate, recognise and take considered action ■ Communication, recording and reporting, i.e. distinction between observation, fact and opinion ■ Personal skills – confidence to challenge, self-awareness Knowledge: ■ Legal and procedural frameworks ■ Wider context of services ■ Self-knowledge, i.e. know how to cope with distress and conflict	Skills: ■ Information handling, i.e. make good use of information and assess relevance and status of information ■ Clear communication – be unambiguous with others ■ Engagement gaining trust and respect Knowledge: ■ Importance of information sharing ■ Role and responsibilities – professional boundaries: how to share information, with whom and when ■ Awareness of complexities of different types of information, cultural diversity ■ Awareness of laws and legislation, i.e. Data Protection Act, confidentiality

Quality Standards for SEN support and outreach services

These standards have a strong focus on strengthening inclusion. The standards apply to all local authority SEN advisory and support services, irrespective of how they are provided. They also apply to, and include, outreach provided by special and mainstream schools, and by voluntary sector services.

The role of teachers and other staff working in SEN support and outreach services is to:

- understand the nature of pupils' difficulties and be able to provide new insights to overcome difficulties;
- understand the school systems that best promote the achievement and inclusion of pupils with SEN;
- have a good understanding of the curriculum modifications and adaptations that secure broad, balanced and relevant opportunities for pupils with SEN;
- promote strategies that can be used in mainstream classrooms;
- have an understanding of pupils' learning styles and how they can be accommodated in the school;
- have good interpersonal skills and promote change within a school;
- monitor the progress of pupils and evaluate the outcomes for pupils, i.e. their achievement, learning, participation and enjoyment, in relation to the additional support provided by the service;
- gather and seek parents'/carers' and pupils' views in evaluating provision;
- respond to any concerns from parents/carers and pupils promptly;
- respond to the needs of particular schools within a Networked Learning Community, complementing other provision in the local area. (DfES 2005e)

The best support from local authority outreach and support services includes coaching for teachers in mainstream schools through demonstrating effective strategies, and providing information on particular special needs or disabilities to staff in schools.

Professional standards for higher level teaching assistants

The standards for HLTAs are informed by the Qualified Teacher Status (QTS) standards. These standards cover three main areas:

1. Professional values and practice:

- Have high expectations, respect and value pupil diversity, with a commitment to raising educational achievement.
- Build and maintain successful relationships with pupils.
- Model and promote positive values, attitudes and behaviour.
- Work collaboratively with other colleagues.
- Liaise sensitively and effectively with parents/carers.
- Improve own practice through observation, evaluation and discussion with colleagues.

2. Knowledge and understanding:

- Have sufficient understanding of their specialist area to support pupils' learning.
- Be familiar with school curriculum, age-related expectations of pupils, main teaching methods and strategies as well as the testing and examination frameworks.
- Know how to use and apply ICT to advance pupils' learning.

- Know key factors that can affect the way pupils learn.
- Know the meaning of SEN and be familiar with guidance in the SEN Code of Practice.
- Know a range of strategies to establish a purposeful learning environment and to promote good behaviour in pupils.

3. Teaching and learning activities

The following teaching and learning activities should take place under the direction and supervision of a qualified teacher.

3.1 Planning and expectations:

- Contribute to teacher planning and lesson preparation.
- Plan their role in lessons within the framework set by the teacher, and provide feedback to pupils and teachers on pupils' learning and behaviour.
- Contribute to the selection and preparation of effective teaching resources to meet the diversity of pupils' needs and interests.
- Contribute to the planning of opportunities for pupils to engage in out-of-hours learning activities.

3.2 Monitoring and assessment:

- Support teachers in evaluating pupils' progress through a range of assessment activities.
- Monitor pupils' responses to learning tasks and modify their approach as necessary.
- Monitor pupils' participation and progress, feeding back to teachers, and giving constructive support to pupils as learners.
- Maintain and analyse records of pupils' progress.

3.3 Teaching and learning activities:

- Interest, motivate and advance pupils' learning through the use of clearly structured teaching and learning activities.
- Communicate effectively and sensibly with pupils to support their learning.
- Promote and support the inclusion of all pupils in learning activities.
- Use appropriate behaviour management strategies in line with the school's policy and procedures.
- Advance pupils' learning through working with individual pupils, small groups and whole class.
- Guide the work of other adults supporting teaching and learning in the classroom, where relevant, e.g. teaching assistants.
- Challenge stereotypical views, bullying or harassment among pupils following relevant policies and procedures relating to equal opportunities.
- Organise and manage safely the learning activities, the physical teaching space and resources for which they have responsibility.

The DfES (2004i: 4) states:

> School support staff, when undertaking specified work, must be subject to the direction and supervision of a teacher in accordance with arrangements made by the headteacher of the school. The headteacher must be satisfied that support staff have the skills, expertise and experience to carry out a range of activities at different levels – including, for some staff, working with whole classes.

Table 6.4 Key roles of Advanced Skills Teachers and Excellent Teachers

ADVANCED SKILLS TEACHERS	EXCELLENT TEACHERS
■ Act as a link to other schools, colleges and educational bases	■ Play a significant part in the development of new school policies
■ Be able to apply skills and techniques gleaned from other schools to own school	■ Promote links with parents and carers
■ Advise teachers and staff in other schools and educational bases on the most effective way to get the most out of pupils	■ Help set training targets for other teachers
■ Act as a change champion	■ Have good knowledge of different teaching styles and advise others on them
■ Advise and support other teachers on planning, teaching, assessment, managing pupils and maintaining classroom discipline	■ Know how to coach and mentor colleagues on work with talented and special needs pupils
■ Demonstrate and model inclusive classroom practice	■ Monitor and evaluate the arrangements set up to track pupil progress
■ Produce high quality teaching and learning resources	■ Act as a lead learner
■ Support and promote the identification and removal of barriers to learning	
■ Disseminate best practice and expertise across schools through networks	

The role of the Learning Mentor

Learning Mentors support schools in raising standards, specifically through raising targeted pupils' achievements, breaking down barriers to learning, improving attendance and reducing exclusions. They bridge the academic and pastoral domains in schools, with the aims of ensuring pupils engage more effectively in learning, achieve appropriately and are socially included.

Learning Mentors work with the full ability range of underachieving pupils, e.g. truants, disaffected and disengaged learners, those facing difficulties at home, those with behaviour problems or those being bullied. Within the context of *Every Child Matters*, Learning Mentors work in an extended range of networks and partnerships to broker support and learning opportunities and improve the quality of services to children and young people.

The contributions that Learning Mentors make to whole-school inclusion processes are significant, particularly in relation to teaching and learning, improving pupil behaviour, attendance, self-esteem and motivation towards study, and helping to celebrate diversity. It is important that the teacher is aware of the Learning Mentor's new and changing role in view of *Every Child Matters*.

Teaching assistants

Teaching assistants (TAs) or learning support assistants (LSAs) are those additional supporting adults who work alongside teachers in the classroom, helping pupils and teachers. How TAs are used is a matter for individual schools. General tasks range from maintaining and organising the layout and availability of equipment in classrooms, arranging displays of work, and helping

Table 6.5 Learning Mentors' role in relation to the five *Every Child Matters* outcomes

Be healthy	Stay safe	Enjoy and achieve	Make a positive contribution	Achieve economic and social well-being
Support schools to achieve Healthy School Standard	Bullying prevention programmes and strategies	Supporting learning and participation through one-to-one and group work	Work with pupil councils	Supporting exam success/qualifications
Breakfast clubs	Encouraging and modelling positive play including peaceful playground projects	Supporting engagement with school	Peer support programmes (including peer mentoring and peer buddying)	Programmes to help pupils prepare for Further Education and employment
Support for making positive choices				Progression planning
After-school clubs (including sports and dance)	Making positive choices	Work with education welfare to support attendance	Bullying prevention programmes and strategies	Raising motivation and aspirations
Sexual health and relationship support	Contributing to drugs education programmes	Programmes to support personal and social development	Programmes to enable pupils to support the environment and their communities (e.g. Prince's Trust and award schemes)	Employability skills
Supporting pupils with mental health difficulties	Child protection work	Study support and study skills programmes		Study support programmes supporting exam success
Being a proactive factor and building pupils' resilience	Family liaison	Work with families, parents and carers, including family learning programmes	Programme to develop confidence and self-esteem	Progression planning
Supporting pupils experiencing bereavement and loss	Multi-agency links (education welfare, youth offending teams, social services, police, tier 1, 2 and 3 health and social care providers, community and voluntary sector, school teaching and support staff)	Homework clubs/summer schools	Programmes to support social and emotional aspects of learning	
Multi-agency links (CAMHS, education welfare, health, social services)		Support transfer and transition		
Developing confidence and self-esteem				
Working with families				

children with their reading and mathematics, on a one-to-one basis or in a small group, through to assisting the teacher in making the curriculum accessible to pupils.

Behaviour and Education Support Teams

Behaviour and Education Support Teams (BESTs) are multi-agency teams, comprising practitioners from health, social care and education. BEST aims to promote emotional well-being, positive behaviour and good school attendance, by identifying and supporting children with, or at risk of developing, emotional and behavioural problems. BEST intervenes and works early with children aged from 5 to 18, their families and schools, in order to prevent emotional and behavioural problems developing further.

Child and Adolescent Mental Health Services (CAMHS)

CAMHS refers to the broad concept of all services that contribute in some way to the mental health care of children and young people, whether provided by health, education, social services or other voluntary organisations. It embraces universal services, such as those provided by GPs, school nurses and social workers, as well as more specialist services dedicated solely to the treatment of children with mental health problems. CAMHS covers all types of provision and intervention from mental health awareness raising and prevention, specialist community-based services, through to an in-patient care for children and young people with mental illness.

Lead professional

The lead professional is the adult who has the most frequent and regular contact with the child, young person and their parents/carers. Lead professionals will usually come from health, social services or education, e.g. they may be a Connexions Personal Adviser, an Education Welfare Officer, a Youth Worker, a Nursery Nurse, Health Visitor, School Nurse, Community Children's Nurse, Substance Misuse Worker or a Family Worker.

The lead professional may also be a member of staff from within a school, e.g. a Pastoral Leader, Learning Mentor, SENCO or a Child Protection Officer. Lead professionals may change over time as the needs of the children or young people change. They will be the professional most relevant to the child's support plan, with the skills to carry out the role effectively. They act as a single point of contact for the child and family, helping to reduce overlap or inconsistency between multi-agencies.

Lead professionals use the Common Assessment information to assist them in co-ordinating the relevant service provision for the child. They act as a gatekeeper for information sharing. Lead professionals support the child, young person and their parents/carers in making their own decisions about provision, and expressing their views on the effectiveness of interventions and service.

Lead professionals act as a 'sounding-board', for the child, young person and their parents/carers. They monitor the overall progress of the child and young person and the impact of additional interventions and support on the child's outcomes. They co-ordinate and lead multi-professional meetings. The role of the lead professional is extremely time consuming, and where school staff are likely to take on such a role, this will need to be built into job descriptions, with sufficient flexible time being made available.

Key worker

The term 'key worker' refers to a lead support and advocacy role provided by practitioners who may come from a number of different agencies, i.e. health, social services or education, for children and young people with more complex needs and disabilities. Key workers in this instance provide:

- a single point of reference for information;
- help in identifying the needs of the child and family;

- a regular review of support arrangements in the context of growing an understanding of a child's abilities and needs;
- regular, long-term contact and continuity of support;
- a means to co-ordinate support from different agencies;
- mediation between school and the family of a disabled child;
- personal or emotional support, sensitive to needs and family circumstances;
- help to enable families to access and receive relevant services;
- help for families to look forward to the child's next stage of development and anticipate service needs;
- a role in implementing the Family Service plan for the child and family.

Key workers for disabled children are often skilled, specialist staff with a limited caseload, which enables the child and family to be supported long term, emotionally and practically. They assume a responsibility for co-ordinating and facilitating the total care package.

'Key worker' can also refer to a practitioner acting in more of a mentoring or befriending role with a child or young person at risk of exclusion or underachievement, e.g. within the Behaviour Improvement Programme (BIP). The role of the key worker in this context is focused on developing a trusting relationship with the child or young person, rather than having a key 'delivery' role.

Teachers working in partnership with parents

The most powerful influence on any child's learning and progress is the support and commitment they receive from their parents (including guardians, foster parents and others in a parenting role). On average, children spend 87 per cent of their time in a school year at home with their parents. Parental involvement in their child's schooling between the ages of 7 and 16 is a more powerful force than family background, size of family and the level of parental education.

Parents and the family are the prime educators before a child attends nursery or starts school, and they remain a major influence in their children's learning through school years and beyond. Parental involvement is usually on two levels: general involvement in supporting the life of the school, and/or supporting the individual child at home and at school with his/her learning. The five *Every Child Matters* outcomes for children will be better and the impact on their learning will also be greater when parents, schools and teachers work in partnership. Both parents and teachers have the child's best interests at heart. Clear communication and mutual respect help to promote positive productive working relationships between the two partners.

The government's White Paper *Higher Standards, Better Schools for All* (DfES 2005j) emphasises the importance of parental engagement throughout a child's education, with the expectation that:

- parents receive high quality information at least three times a year, about what their child is learning, how well they are progressing, areas for further development and how they can support their child's further progress;
- parents will be able to access wider information about their child while they are at school, e.g. whether the child is registered in lessons, information on behaviour and rewards, in addition to academic progress;
- parents are provided with a single point of contact at the school in relation to home–school communication and queries;
- parents are made to feel welcome at the school via its inclusive culture, ethos and approachable communication system, which offers opportunities for regular face-to-face discussions with staff;

- parents will receive home–school agreements which make explicit how schools and parents will work in partnership together;
- parents will be provided with tailored information when their child starts primary school and makes the transition to secondary school;
- parents are encouraged by governing bodies to express their views via the Parents Council, in relation to matters concerning the running of the school and prompting change;
- parents are enabled to complain to OFSTED, after following school and local authority complaints procedures, about inadequate standards, where these have not been resolved.

Guidance for teachers on working in partnership with parents:

- Deal with any parental enquiries (written or by telephone) promptly, seeking advice from other senior colleagues if issues are too complex to resolve immediately.
- Utilise the parents' preferred means of communication to relate good news or express concerns.
- Ensure that any written information to parents on aspects of school life and activities or curriculum is produced in jargon-free, parent-friendly, alternative formats, especially for those with disabilities, and for those whose home first language is not English.
- Always listen carefully to what parents say about their children in relation to their learning, behaviour, well-being and additional educational needs, and use this information to guide the child's personalised learning.
- Remember that the insights and opinions parents have about their child are just as valuable and important as those of teachers and other professionals.
- Find out if the parents of children in your class have any particular talents or interests that could be utilised as part of supervised out-of-hours learning activities or after-school clubs in the extended school.
- Reassure parents of the benefits of helping their child with their learning and encourage networking with other parents.

Questions for teachers on strengthening parent partnership:

- Have you asked parents what they expect from the school and teachers?
- What do you expect from parents in relation to them supporting their child's learning, behaviour and well-being?
- How can you involve parents more productively in supporting and taking a greater interest in their child's learning?
- What can you do to establish an effective working relationship with the parents who are anxious or reluctant to engage with the school?
- What can you do to assist parents to help their child with their learning at home?
- How can you contribute to making parents feel more confident in approaching the school for help?
- What opportunities could you create, either alone or in collaboration with other staff, for Family Learning, or Parent Education Classes and Workshops?
- How will you seek the views of parents of children in your class, in relation to their satisfaction or otherwise, with what you and the school provide for their children?

The Economic and Social Research Council study (1999), which focused on children's experiences and perspectives on parental involvement at home and at school in their education, indicated that children wanted their home lives to remain private and kept separate from school life, unless their education was likely to be adversely affected. School life was equated with rules, timetables and mixing with peers, while home life was equated with support and relaxation.

Further activities for teachers

The questions below are designed to promote further discussion and identify ways forward in meeting the *Every Child Matters* agenda in schools, in promoting effective collaborative multi-professional working.

- How has your involvement with members of the paraprofessional team contributed to improving the *Every Child Matters* five outcomes for children and young people?
- What has been the impact of the additional support and interventions from paraprofessionals on the outcomes for targeted pupils?
- How has your planning recognised and taken account of the role of the other paraprofessionals?
- How do you acknowledge and feed back on the contributions of paraprofessionals working in your classroom?
- What contributions can you make at multi-professional team meetings or joint planning meetings to improve the delivery of personalised learning for pupils in your class?
- What experiences and ideas do you bring to multi-disciplinary working in an extended school?
- What further support do you require in order to enable you to contribute to out-of-hours learning activities in an extended school?
- How do you use and act on the feedback you receive from other colleagues working in a paraprofessional team?
- What areas have you identified for further professional development in respect of the *Every Child Matters* Change for Children programme?

Glossary

Academy – is a privately sponsored school replacing a poor performing comprehensive school in a deprived area that has freedom from local authority control.

Additional needs – describes all children at risk of poor outcomes in relation to *Every Child Matters* five outcomes for children and young people, and who require extra support from education, health or social services for a limited time or on a longer-term basis.

Agency – a statutory or voluntary organisation where staff, who are paid or unpaid, work with or have access to children, young people and families.

Assessment for learning – identifies strengths and weaknesses of individual children and helps to track pupil progress, set individual learning targets, tackle underperformance, provide structured feedback to pupils, inform teacher planning, and actively engage learners in self-assessing their learning and progress.

At risk – a term used to describe a child believed and thought to be at risk of significant harm, social exclusion or offending, who requires protection from the local authority and services/agencies.

Behavioural, emotional and social difficulties – describes those pupils of any ability whose behaviour, emotional and social difficulties present a barrier to learning and participation.

Bureaucracy – administrative activities, or other activities, which do not relate directly to the delivery of an effective education for pupils, and which would be reduced by the use of ICT.

Change – a process designed to improve practice, introduce new policies and functions and alter the existing status quo.

Child – is a person under the age of 18. The term 'children and young people' is also used as a 'catch-all' phrase to cover this age group.

Children's Centres – Sure Start provisions open from dawn to dusk providing seamless, holistic, personalised, integrated wraparound care, education and services and support for children under five, and their parents, in order to improve the life chances of children.

Children's trusts – bring together all services for children and young people in an area in order to improve outcomes.

Colleagues – refers to all those professionals with whom a teacher may have a professional relationship. They may include teaching colleagues, teaching assistants, and the wider Children's Workforce from education, health and social services, working with teachers within an educational setting.

Commissioning – is a process of changing things, particularly by spending money differently, in order to achieve better outcomes and results for people.

Common Assessment Framework – a holistic assessment tool used by the whole children's workforce to assess the additional needs of children and young people at the first signs of difficulties.

Concern – a suspicion or a belief that a child may be in need of help or protection.

Contextual value added – compares the progress made by each pupil with the average progress made by similar pupils in similar schools.

Disabled – any individual who has a physical or mental impairment, which has a substantial and long-term adverse effect on his/her ability to carry out normal day-to-day activities. The definition also covers pupils with sensory or intellectual impairments, those with a learning disability, or who are incontinent, or who have AIDS, severe disfigurements or progressive conditions like muscular dystrophy.

Early Years – refers to children or provision for children within the age range of 0 to 7. It is also used to refer to the pre-reception years, or under-fives, or to those settings such as nurseries and Children's Centres where pre-school children are cared for and educated.

Engagement – involving the customer/user (children, young people and families) in the design and delivery of services and decisions that affect them.

Evaluation – is concerned with gauging effectiveness, strengths and weaknesses, and interpreting how well things are going.

Extended schools – offer a range of services and activities, often beyond the school day, to help meet the needs of children, young people and their families, and the wider community.

Federation – refers to a group of two or more schools with a formal agreement to work together to raise standards.

Foundation Stage – is a distinct phase of education for children aged 3 to 5, which provides a framework for children's learning in nursery or reception class.

Inclusion – describes the process of ensuring equality of learning opportunities for all children and young people, irrespective of their diversity (disabilities or disadvantages). It is about the quality of pupils' experience, how they are helped to learn, achieve and participate fully in the life of the school and within the community.

Information sharing – passing on relevant information to other agencies, organisations and individuals that require it in order to deliver better services to children and young people.

Key worker – refers to a practitioner from health, social services or education who provides a lead support and advocacy role to children and young people with more complex needs.

Lead professional – a designated professional (from health, social services or education), who has day-to-day contact with a child/young person, and who co-ordinates and monitors service provision, acting as a gatekeeper for information sharing.

Learners – as an inclusive term refers to all children and young people, including those with special or additional learning needs.

Looked after child – refers to any child who is in care of the local authority, or who is provided with accommodation by the local authority social services department for a continuous period of more than 24 hours. The term also covers children subject to accommodation under a voluntarily agreed series of short-term placements like short breaks, family link placements or respite care.

Monitoring – checking progress against targets, looking out for trends in performance indicators and seeing that strategies have been implemented.

Multi-agency working – refers to agencies, organisations and individuals working together.

National Service Framework – provides a set of quality standards for health, social care and some education services, and is aimed at reducing inequalities in service provision, in order to improve the lives and health of children and young people.

Out-of-hours learning – refers to any club or organised activity that children and young people attend outside normal classroom time, e.g. lunch time, before and after school, during school holidays.

Outcomes – refers to the identifiable (positive or negative) impact of interventions, programmes or services on children and young people. It also refers to the five *Every Child Matters* outcomes.

Paraprofessional – any individual with some kind of knowledge and training who performs important service delivery activities to remove barriers to learning, achievement and participation, and who works as part of a multi-disciplinary team within one or across a range of educational settings.

Peer support – is about making pupils feel safe and supported by other pupils within the school in order to address individual problems such as bullying, making friendships and school transition.

Personalised learning – embraces every aspect of school life including teaching and learning strategies, ICT, curriculum choice, organisation and timetabling, assessment arrangements and relationships with the local community.

Practitioner – refers to anyone who works directly with children and young people and their families, whose primary role is to use a particular expertise or professional skill to help promote children's and young people's well-being.

Remodelling – is a self-directed approach that places the school in control to diagnose its own issues, choose what to work on and to make change happen.

Safeguarding – describes the process of identifying children and young people who have suffered or who are likely to suffer significant harm, and then taking the appropriate action to keep them safe.

Specialist services – include child protection services, adoption and fostering services for looked after children and their families, residential services, and services for children with serious mental health problems such as eating disorders. These services are provided specifically for children with acute or high level needs who would otherwise be at a high risk of achieving poor outcomes.

Sure Start – established in 1999, refers to the extensive government programme to eradicate child poverty in the most deprived areas, with the aim of improving the health and well-being of families and children from before birth to the age of four. Sure Start local programmes became Children's Centres in 2006.

Targeted services – provide support for children less likely to achieve optimal outcomes who have additional needs, or complex needs, ideally within universal settings such as Children's Centres and Full-Service Extended Schools.

Transition – refers to the number of changes and stages a child and young person will pass through during their educational career, as they grow and develop, e.g. primary to secondary school, from Children's Services to Adult Services.

Universal services – also known as mainstream services, are provided and made routinely available to all children, young people and their families, which includes Early Years provision, mainstream schools and Connexions, GP, midwives and health visitors.

Vulnerable children – refers to those children at risk of social exclusion, those who are disadvantaged and whose life chances are likely to be jeopardised unless action is taken to meet their needs better.

Welfare – refers to child safety issues and child protection.

Well-being – refers to the five *Every Child Matters* outcomes for children and young people: being healthy, staying safe, enjoying and achieving, making a positive contribution, achieving economic and social well-being.

Workplace – refers to the range of educational establishments and settings where teaching takes place, which encompasses the outreach role of Advanced Skills Teachers.

Young person – is defined as someone aged 14–17 years, but also refers to those aged 18–25. Most policy documents use the term 'children and young people'.

Useful Websites

www.ascl.org.uk

www.childline.org.uk

www.childrenscommissioner.org

www.dfes.gov.uk

www.direct.gov.uk

www.drc.org.uk/education

www.everychildmatters.gov.uk

www.gtce.org.uk

www.naht.org.uk

www.ncsl.org.uk

www.ofsted.gov.uk

www.qca.org.uk

www.remodelling.org

www.standards.dfes.gov.uk

www.standards.dfes.gov.uk/federations

www.standards.dfes.gov.uk/innovation-unit

www.standards.dfes.gov.uk/innovation-unit/personalisation

www.standards.dfes.gov.uk/personalisedlearning/presentations

www.surestart.gov.uk

www.tda.gov.uk

www.teachernet.gov.uk

www.teachers.org.uk

References and Further Reading

ATL (2002) *Achievement for All: Working with Children with Special Educational Needs in Mainstream Schools and Colleges*. London: Association of Teachers and Lecturers.

Bond, Kate and Waterhouse, Joanne (2005) *Building New Relationships in a Networked Landscape*. NCSL conference. London: National College of School Leadership.

Cheminais, R. (2001) *Developing Inclusive School Practice: A Practical Guide*. London: David Fulton Publishers.

Cheminais, R. (2002) *Special Educational Needs for Newly Qualified and Student Teachers: A Practical Guide*. London: David Fulton Publishers.

Cheminais, R. (2004) *How to Create the Inclusive Classroom: Removing Barriers to Learning*. London: David Fulton Publishers.

Cheminais, R. (2005) *Every Child Matters: A New Role for SENCOs. A Practical Guide*. London: David Fulton Publishers.

ChildLine (2002) *Information Sheet 10: Rights of Children and Young People*. London: ChildLine.

ChildLine (2005) *Every School Should Have One: How Peer Support Schemes Make Schools Better*. London: ChildLine.

CSIE (2002) *Index for Inclusion: Developing Learning and Participation in Schools*. Bristol: Centre for Studies on Inclusive Education.

DfES (2001a) *Advanced Skills Teachers: Promoting Excellence*. London: Department for Education and Skills.

DfES (2001b) *Good Practice Guidelines for Learning Mentors*. London: Department for Education and Skills.

DfES (2002b) *An Introduction to Extended Schools Providing Opportunities and Services for All*. London: Department for Education and Skills.

DfES (2003a) *Every Child Matters: Summary*. London: Department for Education and Skills.

DfES (2003b) *The Impact of Parental Involvement on Children's Education*. London: Department for Education and Skills.

DfES (2003c) *Together from the Start: Practical Guidance for Professionals Working with Disabled Children (Birth to Third Birthday) and their Families*. London: Department for Education and Skills.

DfES (2004a) *Assessment for Learning: Whole School Training Materials. Primary National Strategy*. London: Department for Education and Skills.

DfES (2004b) *Building Schools for the Future: Local Authority Education Vision. Policy Guidelines for Wave 2*. London: Department for Education and Skills.

DfES (2004c) *Developing the Role of School Support Staff: What the National Agreement Means for You.* London: Department for Education and Skills.

DfES (2004d) *Every Child Matters: Change for Children.* London: Department for Education and Skills.

DfES (2004e) *Every Child Matters: Change for Children in Schools.* London: Department for Education and Skills.

DfES (2004f) *Every Child Matters: Next Steps.* London: Department for Education and Skills.

DfES (2004g) *Excellence and Enjoyment: Learning and Teaching in the Primary Years. Introductory guide: Continuing Professional Development.* London: Department for Education and Skills.

DfES (2004h) *Five Year Strategy for Children and Learners.* London: Department for Education and Skills.

DfES (2004i) *Guidance for Schools on Higher Level Teaching Assistant Roles for School Support Staff.* London: Department for Education and Skills.

DfES (2004j) *National Occupational Standards for Learning Development and Support Services.* London: Department for Education and Skills.

DfES/DH (2004k) *National Service Framework for Children, Young People and Maternity Services: Executive Summary.* London: Department for Education and Skills.

DfES (2004m) *Removing Barriers to Achievement: The Government's Strategy for SEN.* London: Department for Education and Skills.

DfES (2004n) *Safeguarding Children in Education.* London: Department for Education and Skills.

DfES (2004o) *School Profile Consultation.* London: Department for Education and Skills.

DfES (2004p) *Smoking Out Underachievement: Guidance and Advice to Help Secondary Schools Use Value Added Approaches with Data.* London: Department for Education and Skills.

DfES (2004q) *Strategies for Improving Schools: A Handbook for School Improvement Partners.* London: Department for Education and Skills.

DfES (2004r) *A Ten Year Strategy for Childcare.* London: Department for Education and Skills.

DfES (2005a) *Children's Trusts.* London: Department for Education and Skills.

DfES (2005b) *Common Assessment Framework for Children and Young People: Guide for Service Managers and Practitioners.*

DfES (2005c) *Common Assessment Framework for Children and Young People: Impact Assessment.* London: Department for Education and Skills.

DfES (2005d) *Common Core of Skills and Knowledge for the Children's Workforce.* London: Department for Education and Skills.

DfES (2005e) *Draft Standards for SEN Support and Outreach Services.* London: Department for Education and Skills.

DfES (2005f) *Education Improvement Partnerships, Local Collaboration for School Improvement and Better Service Delivery.* London: Department for Education and Skills.

DfES (2005g) *Every Child Matters: Glossary.* London: Department for Education and Skills.

DfES (2005h) *Every Child Matters: Outcomes Framework.* London: Department for Education and Skills.

DfES (2005i) *14–19 Education and Skills: Summary*. London: Department for Education and Skills.

DfES (2005j) *Higher Standards, Better Schools for All: More Choice for Parents and Pupils*. London: Department for Education and Skills.

DfES (2005k) *Information Sharing (IS) Index: Fact Sheet*. London: Department for Education and Skills.

DfES (2005l) *Lead Professional Good Practice Guidance for Children with Additional Needs*. London: Department for Education and Skills.

DfES (2005m) *Leading on Inclusion: Primary National Strategy*. London: Department for Education and Skills.

DfES (2005o) *Promoting Inclusion and Tackling Underperformance: Maximising Progress. Ensuring the Attainment of Pupils with SEN*. Key Stage 3 National Strategy. London: Department for Education and Skills.

DfES (2005p) *A Quick Guide to Common Assessment*. London: Department for Education and Skills.

DfES (2005q) *Supporting the New Agenda for Children's Services and Schools: The Role of Learning Mentors and Co-ordinators*. London: Department for Education and Skills.

DfES (2005r) *Teachers: Special Report. A Guide to the New White Paper: Higher Standards, Better Schools for All*. London: Department for Education and Skills.

DfES (2005s) *Working in an Academy: A Guide*. London: Department for Education and Skills.

DfES (2004l) *A New Relationship with Schools*. London: Department for Education and Skills.

DfES/OFSTED (2005b) *A New Relationship with Schools: Next Steps*. London: Department for Education and Skills/Office for Standards in Education.

DRC (2002) *A Guide for Schools: Part 4 of the Disability Discrimination Act 1995 as Amended by the Special Educational Needs and Disability Act 2001*. Coventry: Disability Rights Commission.

DRC (2005) *The Duty to Promote Disability Equality: Statutory Code of Practice – England and Wales*. Coventry: Disability Rights Commission.

Education Extra (2005) *Parent Extra Guide to Out-of-School-Hours Learning*. London: Education Extra.

Edwards, R., David, M. and Aldred, P. (1999) *Parental Involvement in Education: Children and Young People's Views*. Swindon: Economic and Social Research Council.

Fidler, B. (2002) *Strategic Management for School Development: Leading Your School's Improvement Strategy*. London: Paul Chapman Publishing.

GTC (2003) *The Teachers' Professional Learning Framework*. London: General Teaching Council.

Hargreaves, D. (2003) *Working Laterally: How Innovation Networks Make an Education Epidemic*. London: Department for Education and Skills.

IRSC (2004) *Training Material for School Support Staff and Teaching Assistants*. Sussex: National Network of Investigation and Referral Support Co-ordinators.

Lancashire County Council (2005) *Assessment of Learning, Performance Monitoring and Effective Target Setting 3 for all Pupils*. Preston: Lancashire Professional Development Service.

Last, G. (2004) *Personalised Learning: Adding Value to the Learning Journey Through the Primary School.* London: Department for Education and Skills.

Lindsey, J.D. (1983) 'Paraprofessionals in learning disabilities', *Journal of Learning Disabilities,* **16**(8).

MacBeath, J. (2005) *School Self-Evaluation: Background, Principles and Key Learning.* Nottingham: National College for School Leadership/Secondary Headteachers Association.

NAHT (2002) *Primary Leadership Paper 1.* London: National Association of Headteachers.

NCSL (2002/2003) *Leading and Managing Staff. NPQH Development Module 3, D1 Strategic Direction and Development of the School, Change and the Individual.* Nottingham: National College of School Leadership.

NCSL (2005b) *What Are We Learning About? Developing a Network Perspective.* Bedfordshire: National College for School Leadership.

NCSL (2005c) *What Are We Learning About? Establishing a Network of Schools.* Bedfordshire: National College for School Leadership.

NCSL (2005d) *What Makes a Network a Learning Network?* Bedfordshire: National College for School Leadership.

NCSL/SHA (2005a) *School Self-Evaluation: A Reflection and Planning Guide for Schools.* Nottingham: National College for School Leadership/Secondary Headteachers Association.

NUT (2005) *OFSTED Inspection Framework: NUT Guidance.* London: National Union of Teachers.

OFSTED (2000) *Evaluating Educational Inclusion: Guidance for Inspectors and Schools.* London: Office for Standards in Education.

OFSTED (2004) *Special Educational Needs and Disability: Towards Inclusive Schools.* London: Office for Standards in Education.

OFSTED (2005a) *The Annual Report of Her Majesty's Chief Inspector of Schools 2004/2005.* London: Office for Standards in Education.

OFSTED (2005b) *Conducting the Inspection: Guidance for Inspectors of Schools.* London: Office for Standards in Education.

OFSTED (2005c) *An Employment-Based Route into Teaching: An Overview of the First Year of the Inspection of Designated Recommended Bodies for the Graduate Teacher Programme 2003/04.* London: Office for Standards in Education.

OFSTED (2005d) *Every Child Matters: Framework for the Inspection of Schools in England from September 2005.* London: Office for Standards in Education.

OFSTED (2005e) *Guidance on the Use of Evidence Forms.* London: Office for Standards in Education.

OFSTED (2005f) *Inclusion: The Impact of LEA Support and Outreach Services.* London: Office for Standards in Education.

OFSTED (2005g) *Self-Evaluation Form for Secondary Schools (with and without Sixth Forms).* London: Office for Standards in Education.

OFSTED (2005h) *Using the Evaluation Schedule: Guidance for Inspectors of Schools.* London: Office for Standards in Education.

QCA/DfEE (1998) *Supporting the Target Setting Process: Guidance for Effective Target Setting for Pupils with Special Educational Needs.* London: Qualifications and Curriculum Authority/Department for Education and Employment.

QCA (2000) *A Language in Common: Assessing English as an Additional Language.* London: Qualifications and Curriculum Authority.

QCA (2001a) *Planning, Teaching and Assessing the Curriculum for Pupils with Learning Difficulties: Personal, Social and Health Education and Citizenship.* London: Qualifications and Curriculum Authority.

QCA (2001b) *Supporting School Improvement: Emotional and Behavioural Development.* London: Qualifications and Curriculum Authority.

SHA (2005) School Profile: SHA Conference. London: Secondary Headteachers Association.

Shaw, M. and Paton, G. (2006) 'More Hurdles to Higher Pay Grades', *Times Educational Supplement*, January 13, p. 4.

TDA (2005) *Consultation on the Review of Standards for Classroom Teachers.* London: Training and Development Agency for Schools.

TTA (2004) *Professional Standards for Higher Level Teaching Assistants.* London: Teacher Training Agency.

TTA (2005) *Corporate Plan 2005–2008.* London: Teacher Training Agency.

Index

LEARNING RESOURCES CENTRE